COFFEE COOKBOOK:

150+ HOMEMADE RECIPES THAT TASTE EXACTLY LIKE AT A COFFEE SHOP! TIPS AND TRICKS TO MAKE THE PERFECT CAPPUCCINO, ICED COFFEE, MOCHA, CHAI ESPRESSO, COOKIES & CREAM, AND MORE

TABLE OF CONTENTS

What are the benefits of making blended coffees at home?

Can you make your coffee enjoyable, beyond the prospect of drinking it when you're finished?

Who could say no, including alcohol, chocolate, fruit, and other great ingredients?

When the weekend rolls around, you probably don't feel like heading out to pick up coffee, especially if it's raining or the weather is cold.

It's not difficult, and once you have stocked up the essential ingredients, you can prepare coffee without making trips to purchase ingredients.

Picture a gloomy day, snuggling up with a good book and sipping coffee that is tailor-made with your favorite tastes. From coffee that has alcohol in it to iced coffees and some with the consistency of a smoothie, there are coffee blends for everyone.

Homemade coffee is the perfect choice on those rainy and cold days when you don't want to wander out. And it will save you money, too. Whether you've made coffee yourself or not, you'll find it's not difficult to do. You'll find some recipes that will become quick favorites, and with 155 recipes to choose from, there will always be new tastes to try, too!

The Devices

There are a variety of devices that are used to make great coffee or espresso at home. Some are very simple to use, while others have more intricate features. This section provides an overview of some of the more popular devices and their best use.

Automatic Drip Brewer

The automatic drip brewer is the standard across America for making a quick, classic cup of coffee. Most homes are equipped with one, and they seldom sit unused. The first automatic drip brewer by Mr Coffee hit the market in 1972. By 1974, half of the 10 million coffee makers sold in America were automatic drip brewers. The legacy of this brewer lives on today as a traditional way to make coffee, steeped in family tradition. There is nothing like the sweet sound of a drip machine bubbling as the coffee slowly drips into the carafe, where enough coffee for the entire family can be made. This method is undoubtedly the easiest option for someone on the go, as all you need to do is put the grounds and water in the machine and click START! After five minutes or so, you have an entire pot of coffee! Another plus: This device is sold almost everywhere, ranging in price from $10 to $300. Depending on the features you are looking for. If you are open to a used machine, you can bet on finding multiple choices at any thrift store or yard sale for $1 or $2.

Perfect For

The automatic drip brewer is the best way to brew coffee for a large group. Most machines can make at least 10 to 12 cups at a time (some even more), and it takes only a few minutes. The machines are also very hands-off, which allows you to start the coffee and walk away until it is finished. The only downfall is that these machines are not known for producing exceptional coffee unless you are willing to spend hundreds of dollars to buy one that imitates a manual pour-over. The lower-end models dump water on the grounds at an uncontrolled speed and temperature, which often causes the coffee to be burned and under-extracted, resulting in a less-than-perfect taste.

Manual Pour Over

You would be remiss if you attempted to get into specialty coffee and knew nothing about the manual pour-over. This method had been around since its invention in 1908. However, it has become the most popular specialty coffee brewing method in shops and homes worldwide in recent years. The pour-over is precisely what the name suggests: You pour hot water over coffee grounds held within a filter basket or cone-shaped paper filter. The most popular pour-over devices are the Chemex and the Hario V60 dripper.

The Chemex was invented by Dr Peter Schlumbohm, a chemist (hence the name). It quickly grew in popularity due to its visually striking design and how it could brew coffee using nonporous glass without imparting any flavors of its own into the cup.

It cost between the range of $10 on the low-end plastic and $40 on the high end for glass Chemex coffeepot to acquire a manual pour over on average.

The Hario V60 is very similar in design but can sit atop your mug for easy use and portability. The pour-over method has become so popular among coffee enthusiasts due to the degree of control it gives the barista. It allows you to pour water at a controlled rate and pattern for optimal extraction.

Pour overs are perfect if you have higher-quality coffee with vibrant flavor notes. The pour-over has the unique and unrivalled ability to pull out the coffee beans' sweet and delicate flavors. The downside is that the process can be tricky to master, and first attempts can result in some inconsistently strange cups of coffee. However, once you get the hang of it, the pour-over can produce a well-rounded, gentle, straightforward cup of coffee. Another thing to note with this method is that it is typically not ideal for making coffee in large quantities. There are higher-volume versions of the Chemex, but most pour-overs are geared for 1 to 2 cups at a time and often take a few minutes of your undivided attention for best results. That said, if you are willing to give it the time and effort, it is well worth it!

French Press

Aside from the automatic drip brewer, the French press is one of the most popular home brewing methods around, and for a good reason. Brewing a decent cup of morning coffee on a French press is nearly guaranteed, making it accessible to even the most amateur coffee brewers. The brewing process consists of pouring hot water over the grounds, letting them brew for 3 to 4 minutes, and pressing the metal filter down, pushing the coffee grounds to the bottom of the pitcher. Since 1800, the Immersion method of brewing has been attributed to a Frenchman who forgot to add his coffee to the pot before boiling the water. After adding the grounds to the boiling water, he noticed they floated at the top. Not wanting to waste the precious beverage, the man used a metal screen and a stick to push all the grounds to the bottom of the pot, resulting in a nicely brewed cup of coffee.

Today, the French press is famous for its ease of use and versatility. In addition to brewing hot coffee, this device can make cold brews, tea, and even frothed milk! One negative aspect of using the French press is that there is often a noticeable amount of "sludge" at the bottom of your cup due to the larger holes in the metal filter. However, some people enjoy the thickness that comes from coffee sediment. It's a personal preference. The French press is straightforward to find in stores or online and purchased for $20 to $30.

Perfect For

The French press is an excellent option for those who enjoy a more prosperous, medium-bodied cup of coffee but still need something simple and user-friendly. The French press is easy to use and is something you can start and walk away from for a few minutes, rather than having to tend the coffee meticulously. The French press is an immersion method that often produces more robust, creamy flavors than the pour-over method's fruity, vibrant flavors. The taste can, in many ways, be likened to the rich comfort of a cozy blanket by the fireplace on a snowy winter's eve.

Aeropress

The AeroPress did not hit the market until 2005, making it the newbie of coffee brewing devices. It was developed by an engineer who spent years researching ways to create the best single-serve brewing device. The result is an incredibly smooth cup of coffee made in a fraction of the time other methods can take and with minimal hassle. Its most common use is for making espresso-like coffee. The AeroPress is an immersion brewing method, but the short brewing time comes from a smaller grind size. A plunger was inserted into the device, and trapped air pushes the water through a small paper filter and directly into your cup. The AeroPress is low maintenance, portable, and easy to use. It's a great option to bring along when you travel, as it is small and made of plastic. These brewers can be found online and in many stores and cost about $30. One drawback is that the AeroPress is not an excellent option for making coffee for all your friends, as it is, by nature, a single-serve brewing device.

Perfect For

AeroPress was praised repeatedly for its ability to make espresso-like coffee in such a short amount of time and without all the expensive gear that comes with making espresso. The AeroPress has gained such momentum that there is a World AeroPress Championship each year, where participants compete to make the best espresso using this device in recent years.

Moka Pot

The Moka pot was invented by Luigi di Ponti and Alfonso Bialetti in Italy in 1933 and has been a classic ever since. The Moka pot is a stovetop coffee maker that brews coffee by passing water pressurized by steam through a bed of grounds placed above it. The idea behind the Moka pot was to make espresso at home without the expensive equipment. At the time, it was undoubtedly the best and most affordable alternative! Today, you find many different versions of the Moka pot; however, the Bialetti is made of aluminum and has eight sides for even heat distribution. Although it is no longer at its peak of popularity compared to other brewing methods, it has had a resurgence lately within the specialty coffee community. At roughly $25, its affordability and the aesthetic of a tiny pot of espresso gurgling on the kitchen stove are what draw people back to the timeless classic.

Perfect For

The Moka pot rivals the AeroPress as the most accessible, most affordable home brewing espresso. It produces a full-bodied, sweet, and, often called, "viscous" shot of espresso. It is a fantastic option if you do not have the money to buy a full-out espresso machine. Another convenient attribute of the Moka pot is its small size. It is highly portable and makes any kitchen look supremely "cute" simply by its presence.

Espresso Maker

The espresso machine originated in Italy in the early 1900s. It was brought to the United States in the 1920s and can be found in virtually any coffee shop today. For our purposes, however, we will focus on home espresso makers rather than the large commercial machines found in most coffee shops. Access to an at-home espresso machine has only been a reality for about 20 years. As you might guess, the price point for these machines is on the higher end, averaging several hundred dollars for a good machine. The espresso maker is good for just that: making espresso.

Espresso is made when hot water is quickly forced through finely-ground coffee. It is typically made in "shots" of 1 to 2 ounces. The upside of having a home espresso maker includes quickly creating a variety of espresso drinks that may take more time without an actual machine. In addition, most espresso makers can steam and froth milk, and many can even grind beans. However, keep in mind that most home espresso makers cannot make the same quality espresso as a much more expensive commercial machine, so many people argue it is not worth the money. They also require regular maintenance to keep them in good working condition.

Perfect For

These expensive machines are perfect for those who genuinely love espresso as their daily drink of choice. Most people who own an espresso machine use it to make specialty drinks that require espresso. This device can be in the form of a straight shot of espresso or as a latte, frappe, or cappuccino. The other beauty of the espresso machine is that it is excellent for hosting a crowd, as you will be able to make unique drinks that stand apart from a simple cup of coffee.

The Milk

Many coffee beverages require either steamed or frothed milk. Steamed milk is essentially milk that has been heated. Steaming milk brings out its natural sweetness and creates a slightly thicker texture. Steamed milk is responsible for the creaminess of a latte, among other drinks. Frothed milk has more air whipped into it and, therefore, less liquid and adds a thick layer of foam on top of many beverages, such as a cappuccino.

Milk Frother

A milk frother is a relatively inexpensive device used to create frothed milk. A small handheld milk frother can be purchased for $10 to $15 and quickly and easily makes that foamy goodness you need to top off your homemade cappuccino.

Milk Steamer

A milk steamer is often found on more expensive home espresso makers and requires an additional steaming pitcher for use. Steamers are convenient because they inject air into the milk at high speeds, creating froth while simultaneously heating it. This process saves time and prevents the milk from cooling during the frothing process. However, these machines are much more expensive and less accessible to the average person.

Milk Alternatives

Although whole milk gives the best results when steaming or frothing milk, it is not the only option. Soymilk is a good alternative for getting a creamy texture and thick foam without the dairy. Almond milk offers a sweet, nutty flavor but doesn't thicken up very well when frothed. A newer popular milk alternative in the coffee world is oat milk, which has a milder flavor than almond milk and froths and steams.

BROWN SUGAR COCONUT LATTE

Serving: 1

Preparation Time: 5 minutes

Cooking Time: 10 minutes

Ingredients

- 1/4 cup canned coconut milk
- 1/2 cup unsweetened coconut milk beverage (such as Silk®)
- 1 tbsp. brown sugar
- 1/2 tsp. coconut oil
- 1/4 tsp. coconut extract
- 1 cup strong brewed coffee

Direction

1. Combine coconut extract, coconut oil, brown sugar, coconut milk beverage, and canned coconut milk in a saucepan. Heat till hot over low heat. Froth milk mixture till foamy with an immersion blender.
2. In a large mug, add coconut milk mixture. Use a spoon's back to hold foam back. Add in coffee and top with foam.

Nutrition Information

- Calories: 464 calories;

- Total Carbohydrate: 21.6 g
- Cholesterol: 0 mg
- Total Fat: 43 g
- Protein: 4.2 g
- Sodium: 34 mg

BROWN SUGAR LATTE

Serving: 1

Preparation Time: 2 minutes

Cooking Time: 7minutes

Ingredients

- 1/2 cup milk
- 1 tbsp. caramel sauce
- 1 tbsp. brown sugar
- 1 cup strong brewed coffee

Direction

1. Over medium heat, combine brown sugar, caramel sauce, and milk in a saucepan, and then let it simmer. Use a stick blender to froth the mixture.
2. Add the hot milk mixture into a mug; use a spoon's back to hold back the foam. Add coffee and top with foam.

Nutrition Information

- Calories: 163 calories;
- Total Carbohydrate: 32 g
- Cholesterol: 10 mg
- Total Fat: 2.5 g
- Protein: 4.3 g
- Sodium: 94 mg

COLD BREW AND ALMOND MILK LATTE

Serving: 2

Preparation Time: 5 minutes

Cooking Time: 18h5 minutes

Ingredients

- 4 cups room-temperature water
- 1/2 cup coarsely ground coffee beans
- 2 cups almond milk, or to taste

Direction

1. In a big carafe, combine coffee grounds and water, then stir. Cover and store in the fridge for 12-18 hours or allow to sit at room temperature.
2. Pour the coffee into a bottle through a cheesecloth or a coffee filter to catch the grounds.
3. Fill cold-brewed coffee in an ice cube tray and freeze for 6 hours to overnight till cubes are set. Keep frozen cubes till ready to use in a resealable plastic bag.
4. Fill coffee ice cubes in 1 glass and add almond milk on top.

Nutrition Information

- Calories: 76 calories;
- Total Carbohydrate: 10.9 g
- Cholesterol: 0 mg
- Total Fat: 2.7 g
- Protein: 1.7 g
- Sodium
- 186 mg

WHIPPED BANANA LATTE

Serving: 5

Preparation Time: 10 minutes

Cooking Time: 10 minutes

Ingredients

- 1-1/2 cups cold strong brewed coffee
- 3/4 cup half-and-half cream
- Two medium ripe bananas, frozen
- 1/2 cup ice cubes
- 1/4 cup sugar
- 2 tbsps. chocolate syrup

Direction

1. In a blender, add all ingredients; cover and process till smooth for 15 seconds. Add into chilled glasses and immediately serve.

Nutrition Information

- Calories: 149 calories
- Total Carbohydrate: 27 g
- Cholesterol: 18 mg
- Total Fat: 4 g
- Fiber: 1 g
- Protein: 2 g
- Sodium: 24 mg

ICED COFFEE LATTE

Serving: Makes five servings, 1 cup each.

Preparation Time: 10 minutes

Cooking Time: 10 minutes

Ingredients

- 6 Tbsp. ground MAXWELL HOUSE Coffee, any variety
- 3 cups cold water
- 2 cups milk

Direction

1. Add coffee in filter in coffee maker's brew basket. Pour water in the coffee maker, then brew. Let it be completely calm.
2. Add coffee into a pitcher. Stir in milk till well blended. Store in the fridge till ready to serve or serve immediately.
3. Pour over ice cubes in 5 tall glasses to serve.

Nutrition Information

- Calories: 60
- Total Carbohydrate: 7 g
- Cholesterol: 10 mg
- Total Fat: 2 g
- Fiber: 1 g
- Protein: 4 g
- Sodium: 50 mg
- Sugar: 5 g
- Saturated Fat: 1 g

BROWN SUGAR-CARAMEL LATTE

Serving: 1

Preparation Time: 5 minutes

Cooking Time: 10 minutes

Ingredients

- 1 tbsp. brown sugar
- 1/4 cup half-and-half
- 1 tbsp. caramel ice cream topping
- 3/4 cup hot, brewed coffee

Direction

1. Add brown sugar into half-and-half, then stir till dissolved. Use a small whisk or a milk frother to whip. Pour coffee and add caramel sauce; stir till dissolved. Add frothed half-and-half into the coffee. Serve.

Nutrition Information

- Calories: 184 calories;
- Total Carbohydrate: 29.4 g
- Cholesterol: 23 mg

- Total Fat: 7 g
- Protein: 2.3 g
- Sodium: 104 mg

GREEN TEA LATTE

Serving: 2

Preparation Time: 1m

Cooking Time: 2 minutes

Ingredients

- 1 cup soy milk
- 1 cup water
- 1 tbsp. green tea powder (matcha)
- 2 tbsps. white sugar

Direction

1. Combine sugar, green tea powder, water, and soy milk in a small saucepan. Over medium heat, warm while whisking till foamy and hot. Transfer into mugs. Serve.

Nutrition Information

- Calories: 118 calories;
- Total Carbohydrate: 20.8 g
- Cholesterol: 0 mg
- Total Fat: 2.2 g
- Protein: 4.4 g
- Sodium: 66 mg

SIMPLE MOLTEN ICED CHOCOLATE LATTE

Serving: 2

Preparation Time: 5 minutes

Cooking Time: 5 minutes

Ingredients

- 2 cups strong brewed coffee, cold
- 2 tbsps. chocolate sauce

- 2 tbsps. cream cheese softened
- 1 tbsp. demerara sugar
- 1/4 cup heavy whipping cream
- Four ice cubes, or as desired

Direction

1. In a Ninja(R) Bullet or a blender, combine ice cubes, demerara sugar, cream cheese, chocolate sauce, and coffee. Blend till cream cheese is smooth.

Nutrition Information

- Calories: 216 calories;
- Total Carbohydrate: 15.4 g
- Cholesterol: 57 mg
- Total Fat: 16.3 g
- Protein: 2.4 g
- Sodium: 74 m

VANILLA LATTE

Serving: 1

Preparation Time: 5 minutes

Cooking Time: 6 minutes

Ingredients

- 1 1/4 cups 2% milk
- 2 tbsps. vanilla-flavored syrup
- 1 (1.5 fluid oz.) jigger brewed espresso

Direction

1. In a steaming pitcher, add milk and use the steaming wand to heat to 145-165°F or 65-70°C. Add the steamed milk into the profile, hold back the foam using a spoon—place foam on top. Then, measure the vanilla syrup into an oversized coffee mug and pour in the brewed espresso.

Nutrition Information

- Calories: 261 calories;
- Total Carbohydrate: 41.3 g

- Cholesterol: 24 mg
- Total Fat: 6.1 g
- Protein: 10.1 g
- Sodium: 142 mg

HOMEMADE CARAMEL LATTE

Serving: 1

Preparation Time: 5 minutes

Cooking Time: 8m

Ingredients

- 1/2 cup milk
- 1 tbsp. brown sugar
- 1 tbsp. sugar-free caramel topping
- 1 tbsp. caramel sauce
- 1/4 tsp. vanilla extract
- 1 cup coffee

Direction

1. In a saucepan, combine brown sugar and milk over medium heat. Heat for 3 minutes till it's close to simmering and frothy. Lower heat to low. Mix in vanilla extract and caramel sauce. Stir in coffee.

Nutrition Information

- Calories: 218 calories;
- Total Carbohydrate: 45.6 g
- Cholesterol: 10 mg
- Total Fat: 2.5 g
- Protein: 4.6 g
- Sodium: 165 mg

STOVETOP LATTE

Serving: 2

Preparation Time: 5 minutes

Cooking Time: 10 minutes

Ingredients

- 1-1/3 cups fat-free milk
- Sugar substitute equivalent to 2 tsp. sugar
- 2/3 cup hot strong brewed coffee
- Ground cinnamon or baking cocoa, optional

Direction

1. Combine sugar substitute and milk in a small saucepan. Whisk till steaming and foamy over medium heat. Don't bring to a boil. Slowly place into mugs. Add coffee through the foam. Drizzle with cocoa or cinnamon if preferred.

Nutrition Information

- Calories: 61 calories
- Total Carbohydrate: 9 g
- Cholesterol: 3 mg
- Total Fat: 1 g
- Fiber: 0 g
- Protein: 6 g
- Sodium: 86 mg

QUICK GINGERBREAD LATTE

Serving: 1

Preparation Time: 5 minutes

Cooking Time: 7minutes

Ingredients

- 1/2 cup milk
- 1/2 cup water
- 1 tbsp. white sugar

- 1 tbsp. instant coffee
- One pinch ground ginger
- One pinch of ground cinnamon
- One pinch of ground cloves
- One pinch of ground nutmeg
- 1 tbsp. whipped cream, or more to taste

Direction

1. Put water, milk, coffee, sugar, cinnamon, nutmeg, ginger, and cloves and whisk together in a microwave-safe bowl—place bowl inside the microwave and heat for 2 minutes, or until warmed. Transfer latte to a mug; put whipped cream on top.

Nutrition Information

- Calories: 138 calories;
- Total Carbohydrate: 22.2 g
- Cholesterol: 12 mg
- Total Fat: 3.7 g
- Protein: 4.7 g
- Sodium: 61 mg

QUICK PUMPKIN SPICE LATTE

Serving: 1

Preparation Time: 5 minutes

Cooking Time: 10 minutes

Ingredients

- 1 cup milk, divided
- 1 tbsp. white sugar, or more to taste
- 1 tbsp. pumpkin puree
- 1 tsp. pumpkin pie spice
- 1/2 tsp. vanilla extract
- 1/4 cup brewed espresso

Direction

1. In a small saucepan, whisk vanilla extract, pumpkin pie spice, pumpkin puree, sugar, and 1/2 cup of milk over low heat. Simmer for 5 minutes, then whisk in the leftover 1/2 cup of milk.
2. Discard pulp by pouring milk mixture through a fine-mesh sieve. Bring milk mixture back to the saucepan; simmer and whisk for 2 minutes. Whisk in espresso for 1 minute till foamy.

Nutrition Information

- Calories: 184 calories;
- Total Carbohydrate: 25.4 g
- Cholesterol: 20 mg
- Total Fat: 5.1 g
- Protein: 8.2 g
- Sodium: 110 mg

MOCHA

Serving: 1

Preparation Time: 4 minutes

Cooking Time: 5 minutes

Ingredients

- 1 1/4 cups 2% milk
- 2 tbsps. chocolate syrup
- 1 (1.5 fluid oz.) jigger brewed espresso
- 1 tbsp. sweetened whipped cream (optional)

Direction

1. In a steaming pitcher, add milk and heat to 145-165°F or 65-70°C with the steaming wand. In a large coffee mug, measure chocolate syrup. Brew espresso, then pour into the cup. Add steamed milk to the cup, hold back the foam with a spoon. Place whipped cream on top.

Nutrition Information

- Calories: 266 calories;
- Total Carbohydrate: 39.1 g
- Cholesterol: 27 mg
- Total Fat: 7.2 g
- Protein: 11 g
- Sodium: 162 mg

SKINNY CHOCOLATE MOCHA SHAKE

Serving: 1

Preparation Time: 5 minutes

Cooking Time: 2h5 minutes

Ingredients

- 1 cup Gevalia® Cold Brew Concentrate - House Blend
- One envelope sugar-free instant cocoa mix
- 1/4 cup hot water
- 1/4 cup soy milk
- 2 tbsps. sugar-free chocolate syrup
- One packet sugar substitute (such as Truvia®) (optional)

Direction

1. Add cold brew concentrate in ice cube tray(s). Refrigerate for 2-4 hours till frozen solid.
2. Let hot cocoa mix dissolve in hot water.
3. Add a blender, coffee cubes with sweetener, chocolate syrup, soy milk, and cocoa mixture. Blend for 1-2 minutes till frothy and icy.

Nutrition Information

- Calories: 123 calories;
- Total Carbohydrate: 21 g
- Cholesterol: 3 mg
- Total Fat: 1.5 g
- Protein: 6.3 g
- Sodium: 242 mg

STARBUCKS® MOCHA FRAPPUCCINO® REPLICA

Serving: 6

Preparation Time: 30 minutes

Cooking Time: 1day1h30 minutes

Ingredients

- 6 cups cold water

- 1/2 lb. dark roast ground coffee beans
- cheesecloth
- coffee filters
- 5 cups 1% milk
- 1/2 (14 oz.) can sweeten condensed milk
- 3 tbsps. white sugar
- 1 tsp. white sugar
- 1 tbsp. unsweetened cocoa powder
- 1/2 cup hot tap water

Direction

1. In a 1/2-gallon jar (such as Ball(R)), combine coffee and 6 cups of water till grounds are saturated completely. Let steep at room temperature for one day, occasionally stir.
2. Place the coffee in the fridge and let chill for 1 hour.
3. Top a tall, lidded plastic container with a small colander. Line a 6-in. square of cheesecloth on the colander, then place a coffee filter fitly on top.
4. Add about 1 cup of coffee into the colander until the filter begins to clog. Carefully lift the cheesecloth's corners. Discard the liquid by twisting the filter and cloth. One cup with a new filter each time, drain the leftover liquid. Do the process again with the grounds, filter 1 cup at a time; drain out as much liquid as possible. Store the concentrate in the fridge till ready to serve.
5. In a 1/2-gallon jar, mix condensed milk, 1% milk, and concentrate together.
6. In a bowl of hot tap water, dissolve the cocoa powder and 3 tbsp. Plus 1 tsp of sugar together. Pour over the coffee mixture. Cover and shake the jar well.

Nutrition Information

- Calories: 227 calories;
- Total Carbohydrate: 36.9 g
- Cholesterol: 21 mg
- Total Fat: 4.9 g
- Protein: 10 g
- Sodium: 146 mg

WHITE CHOCOLATE MOCHA

Serving: 1

Preparation Time: 4 minutes

Cooking Time: 5 minutes

Ingredients

- 1 1/4 cups 2% milk
- 2 tbsps. white chocolate-flavored syrup
- 1 (1.5 fluid oz.) jigger brewed espresso
- 1 tbsp. sweetened whipped cream (optional)

Direction

1. In a steaming pitcher, add milk and heat to 145-165°F or 65-70°C with the steaming wand. In a giant coffee mug, measure white chocolate syrup. Brew espresso and pour into a cup. Add the steamed milk to the cup, hold back the foam with a spoon. Add whipped cream on top. Serve.

Nutrition Information

- Calories: 269 calories;
- Total Carbohydrate: 41.6 g
- Cholesterol: 27 mg
- Total Fat: 6.8 g
- Protein: 10.2 g
- Sodium: 146 mg

ICED MEXICAN MOCHA

Serving: 1

Preparation Time: 5 minutes

Cooking Time: 5 minutes

Ingredients

- 4 oz. whole milk
- 1 tbsp. chocolate syrup, or to taste
- One dash of hot pepper sauce
- ice cubes
- 4 oz. Gevalia® Cold Brew Concentrate - House Blend

Direction

1. Combine hot sauce, chocolate syrup, and milk in a glass, then thoroughly stir till mixed.
2. Add ice, then pour over ice with cold brew concentrate in a second glass. Stir in the milk chocolate-chilly mixture till combined.

Nutrition Information

- Calories: 130 calories;
- Total Carbohydrate: 19.3 g
- Cholesterol: 11 mg
- Total Fat: 3.9 g
- Protein: 4.1 g
- Sodium: 112 mg

ICED MOCHA COLA

Serving: 1

Preparation Time: 5 minutes

Cooking Time: 5 minutes

Ingredients

- ice, or as needed
- 1 tbsp. instant coffee granules
- 1 (12 fluid oz.) can or bottle cola-flavored carbonated beverage, or as needed.
- 1 1/2 fluid oz. half-and-half

Direction

1. Fill ice in a tall glass. Put on instant coffee granules and gradually add cola into the glass. Gently add and stir half-and-half into the cola to integrate.

Nutrition Information

- Calories: 217 calories;
- Total Carbohydrate: 41.5 g
- Cholesterol: 17 mg
- Total Fat: 5.2 g
- Protein: 1.6 g
- Sodium: 42 mg

ICED MOCHAS

Serving: 4

Preparation Time: 5 minutes

Cooking Time: 1day5 minutes

Ingredients

- 1 1/2 cups cold coffee
- 2 cups milk
- 1/4 cup chocolate syrup
- 1/4 cup white sugar

Direction

1. Add coffee into the cube tray. Freeze overnight or till solid.
2. Combine sugar, chocolate syrup, milk, and coffee ice cubes in a blender. Blend till smooth. Transfer into glasses to serve.

Nutrition Information

- Calories: 163 calories;
- Total Carbohydrate: 30.4 g
- Cholesterol: 10 mg
- Total Fat: 2.6 g
- Protein: 4.5 g
- Sodium: 65 mg

LOW-CALORIE ROOT BEER MOCHA FRAPPE

Serving: 2

Preparation Time: 10 minutes

Cooking Time: 2h10 minutes

Ingredients

- 1 (12 fluid oz.) can or bottle root beer, cold
- water, or as needed
- 1 1/4 cups skim milk
- 3 tbsps. sugar-free chocolate flavoring syrup (such as Torani®)
- 3 tbsps. sugar-free caramel flavoring syrup (such as Torani®)
- 2 tbsps. instant coffee (such as Folgers®)
- 1 tbsp. imitation vanilla extract
- 1 tsp. artificial sweetener, or to taste

Direction

1. Add root beer into an ice cube tray, then fill the tray with water as needed.
2. Freeze to 2-3 hours till solid.
3. A blender combines sweetener, vanilla extract, instant coffee, caramel syrup, chocolate syrup, milk, and frozen root beer. Blend till smooth.

Nutrition Information

- Calories: 218 calories;
- Total Carbohydrate: 47.2 g
- Cholesterol: 3 mg
- Total Fat: 0.1 g
- Protein: 7.9 g
- Sodium: 106 mg

3-MINUTE MOCHACCINO

Serving: 1

Preparation Time: 5 minutes

Cooking Time: 5 minutes

Ingredients

- 3/4 cup milk
- Six ice cubes
- 1 tbsp. white sugar
- 1 tsp. instant coffee granules
- 1 tsp. cocoa powder, or more to taste
- 1/2 tsp. vanilla extract, or more to taste
- 1 tbsp. chocolate syrup
- 1 tbsp. whipped cream

Direction

1. In a blender, blend vanilla extract, cocoa powder, instant coffee granules, sugar, ice cubes and milk till smooth.
2. Use the chocolate syrup to coat a glass's inner side lightly. Add the coffee mixture to the glass. Serve with whipped cream on top.

Nutrition Information

- Calories: 218 calories;
- Total Carbohydrate: 35.9 g
- Cholesterol: 15 mg
- Total Fat: 5.1 g
- Protein: 7 g
- Sodium: 94 mg

A HEALTHIER MOCHACCINO

Serving: 1

Preparation Time: 15 minutes

Cooking Time: 6h15 minutes

Ingredients

- 3 tbsps. double-strength brewed coffee, or more to taste
- 1 cup milk
- One banana, frozen and chunked
- 1 tbsp. raw sunflower seed kernels
- 1 tbsp. chocolate-flavored protein powder
- 1 tbsp. raw slivered almonds

- 1 tbsp. cocoa powder

Direction

1. Fill an ice cube tray with coffee and freeze for 6 hours overnight till completely frozen.
2. In a blender, blend cocoa, almonds, protein powder, sunflower seed kernels, banana and two coffee ice cubes till smooth.

Nutrition Information

- Calories: 370 calories;
- Total Carbohydrate: 47.1 g
- Cholesterol: 20 mg
- Total Fat: 14.3 g
- Protein: 19 g
- Sodium: 166 mg

AZUCENA'S HOMEMADE MOCHA

Serving: 2

Preparation Time: 5 minutes

Cooking Time: 7minutes

Ingredients

- 1 1/2 cups milk
- Three packets of granular no-calorie sucralose sweetener (such as Splenda®)
- 1 tbsp. cocoa powder
- Four shots of freshly brewed espresso

Direction

1. In a big microwave-safe container, add milk and heat in the microwave for 1-2 minutes till warm.
2. Stir cocoa powder and sweetener to dissolve into warmed milk completely.
3. Follow your espresso machine's directions to froth the milk.
4. Add espresso into the frothed milk mixture and stir.

Nutrition Information

- Calories: 104 calories;
- Total Carbohydrate: 11.4 g
- Cholesterol: 15 mg

- Total Fat: 4.1 g
- Protein: 6.6 g
- Sodium: 84 mg

MOCHA COFFEE COOLER

Serving: 2

Preparation Time: 10 minutes

Cooking Time: 10 minutes

Ingredients

- 1 cup cold strong brewed coffee
- 3/4 cup powdered non-dairy creamer
- 1/3 cup white sugar
- 2 tbsps. unsweetened cocoa powder
- 1/2 tsp. vanilla extract
- 14 cubes ice
- 1 tbsp. vegetable oil
- One 5-second spray of cooking spray

Direction

1. In a blender, place coffee and add ice, vanilla extract, cocoa, sugar, and creamer. Over ice cubes, pour vegetables oil and spray into the blender with cooking spray. Blend for 1 1/2 minutes till smooth.

Nutrition Information

- Calories: 399 calories;
- Total Carbohydrate: 55.7 g
- Cholesterol: 0 mg
- Total Fat: 20.2 g
- Protein: 2.9 g
- Sodium: 72 mg

BLENDED MOCHA DRINK

Serving: 2

Preparation Time: 10 minutes

Cooking Time: 10 minutes

Ingredients

- 3/4 cup brewed espresso
- 1/4 cup sweetened condensed milk
- 1 cup whole milk
- Ten ice cubes, or as needed
- 3 tbsps. chocolate syrup, or more to taste

Direction

1. In a bowl, stir sweetened condensed milk and espresso together. Stir in milk and transfer to a blender. Pour chocolate syrup and ice into the espresso mixture. Blend till smooth.

Nutrition Information

- Calories: 276 calories;
- Total Carbohydrate: 44.7 g
- Cholesterol: 25 mg
- Total Fat: 7.8 g
- Protein: 7.7 g
- Sodium: 133 mg

CAFE MOCHA IN A JAR

Serving: 20

Preparation Time: 5 minutes

Cooking Time: 5 minutes

Ingredients

- 1/2 cup instant coffee granules
- 2 2/3 cups non-fat dry milk powder
- 3/4 cup hot cocoa mix
- 1/4 cup powdered non-dairy creamer

- 1/4 cup confectioners' sugar

Direction

1. Process instant coffee granules in a food processor till it becomes a fine powder.
2. Combine confectioners' sugar, creamer, cocoa mix, milk powder and ground instant coffee till evenly mixed in a bowl—Reserve in an airtight container.

Nutrition Information

- Calories: 92 calories;
- Total Carbohydrate: 15 g
- Cholesterol: 3 mg
- Total Fat: 0.7 g
- Protein: 6.3 g
- Sodium: 112 mg

CHOCOLATE ICED MOCHA

Serving: 1

Preparation Time: 5 minutes

Cooking Time: 6 minutes

Ingredients

- 1 1/4 cups cold coffee, divided
- One envelope low-calorie hot cocoa mix
- ice cubes, or as needed
- 1/2 cup unsweetened almond milk
- 2 tbsps. sugar-free chocolate syrup, or more to taste

Direction

1. Add 1/4 cup of coffee in a mug, then heat for 30 seconds till warm. Combine cocoa mix with the coffee till dissolved.
2. Fill ice cubes in a big glass. Pour almond milk and 1 cup of cold coffee over the ice cubes. Mix in chocolate syrup and cocoa mixture with the coffee and almond milk.

Nutrition Information

- Calories: 105 calories;
- Total Carbohydrate: 16.7 g

- Cholesterol: 3 mg
- Total Fat: 1.8 g
- Protein: 5.2 g
- Sodium: 255 mg

EASY BLENDED MOCHA

Serving: 2

Preparation Time: 5 minutes

Cooking Time: 5 minutes

Ingredients

- 1 cup ice cubes
- 1 cup cold coffee
- 2 tsp. unsweetened cocoa powder
- 1 cup cold water
- 3/4 cup sweetened condensed milk

Direction

1. Blends cocoa powder, coffee, and ice in a blender until there are no big ice chunks. Pour in sweetened condensed milk and water. Blend till smooth.

Nutrition Information

- Calories: 374 calories;
- Total Carbohydrate: 63.5 g
- Cholesterol: 39 mg
- Total Fat: 10.3 g
- Protein: 9.6 g
- Sodium: 156 mg

MAYAN MOCHA POWDER

Serving: 12

Preparation Time: 5 minutes

Cooking Time: 5 minutes

Ingredients

- 2/3 cup nonfat dry milk powder
- 2/3 cup instant coffee granules
- 1 1/3 cups white sugar
- 1/3 cup unsweetened cocoa powder
- 1 1/2 tsp. pumpkin pie spice
- 1/2 tsp. ground cinnamon
- 1/4 tsp. ground red pepper

Direction

1. In a bowl, mix ground red pepper, cinnamon, pumpkin pie spice, cocoa powder, sugar, instant coffee granules and nonfat dry milk powder till thoroughly combined. Keep in a resealable plastic bag or an airtight lidded container.

Nutrition Information

- Calories: 122 calories;
- Total Carbohydrate: 28.2 g
- Cholesterol: 1 mg
- Total Fat: 0.4 g
- Protein: 3.1 g
- Sodium: 37 mg

MIXED MOCHA

Serving: 1

Preparation Time: 4 minutes

Cooking Time: 5 minutes

Ingredients

- 1 1/4 cups 2% milk
- 1 1/2 tbsps. white chocolate-flavored syrup
- 1 1/2 tbsps. chocolate syrup
- 1 (1.5 fluid oz.) jigger brewed espresso
- 1 tbsp. whipped cream (optional)

Direction

1. In a steaming pitcher, add milk and heat to 145-165°F or 65-70°C with the steaming wand. Into an oversized coffee mug, measure chocolate syrup and white chocolate. Brew espresso, then

pour into the cup. Add steamed milk into the cup, hold back the foam with a spoon. Place whipped cream on top.

Nutrition Information

- Calories: 321 calories;
- Total Carbohydrate: 53.2 g
- Cholesterol: 27 mg
- Total Fat: 7.1 g
- Protein: 10.8 g
- Sodium: 163 mg

MOCHA COFFEE

Serving: 1

Preparation Time: 5 minutes

Cooking Time: 10 minutes

Ingredients

- 1 cup hot brewed coffee
- 1 tbsp. unsweetened cocoa powder
- 1 tbsp. white sugar
- 2 tbsps. milk

Direction

1. In a mug, add hot coffee. Stir in milk, sugar, and cocoa.

Nutrition Information

- Calories: 78 calories;
- Total Carbohydrate: 16.9 g
- Cholesterol: 2 mg
- Total Fat: 1.4 g
- Protein: 2.3 g
- Sodium: 18 mg

ORANGE MOCHA

Serving: 1

Preparation Time: 5 minutes

Cooking Time: 5 minutes

Ingredients

- 1 cup brewed coffee
- 2 tbsps. orange juice
- 2 tbsps. milk
- 1 tbsp. white sugar
- 1 tbsp. unsweetened cocoa powder

Direction

1. Stir cocoa powder, sugar, milk, orange juice, and coffee together in a mug until cocoa and sugar dissolve.

Nutrition Information

- Calories: 92 calories;
- Total Carbohydrate: 20.1 g
- Cholesterol: 2 mg
- Total Fat: 1.5 g
- Protein: 2.6 g
- Sodium: 19 mg

PALEO AND KETO ALMOND BUTTER MOCHA FOR TWO

Serving: 2

Preparation Time: 10 minutes

Cooking Time: 10 minutes

Ingredients

- 1 1/2 cups warm almond milk
- 1 tbsp. almond butter
- 2 tbsps. instant espresso powder
- 1 tbsp. unsweetened cocoa powder

- 1/2 tsp. vanilla extract
- 1/2 tsp. stevia powder

Direction

1. In a blender, combine stevia powder, vanilla extract, cocoa powder, espresso powder, almond butter, and almond milk. Mix for about 2 minutes till slightly thickened and well combined. Pour into two mugs; sprinkle with cocoa powder. Serve.

Nutrition Information

- Calories: 115 calories;
- Total Carbohydrate: 11.5 g
- Cholesterol: 0 mg
- Total Fat: 7.1 g
- Protein: 2.8 g
- Sodium: 157 mg

FROSTY CARAMEL CAPPUCCINO

Serving: 2

Preparation Time: 10 minutes

Cooking Time: 10 minutes

Ingredients

- 1 cup half-and-half cream
- 1 cup 2% milk
- 3 tbsps. Plus 2 tsp. caramel ice cream topping, divided
- 2 tsp. instant coffee granules
- 8 to 10 ice cubes
- 4 tbsps. whipped cream in a can

Direction

1. Mix ice cubes, coffee, 3 tbsps. Of caramel topping, milk and half-and-half in a blender. Cover and blend till smooth.
2. Transfer to 2 chilled glasses. Place whipped cream on top and drizzle with the leftover caramel topping. Immediately serve.

Nutrition Information

- Calories: 337 calories
- Total Carbohydrate: 36 g
- Cholesterol: 75 mg

- Total Fat: 16 g
- Fiber: 0 g
- Protein: 9 g
- Sodium: 262 mg

FROSTY MOCHA DRINK

Serving: 4

Preparation Time: 15 minutes

Cooking Time: 15 minutes

Ingredients

- 1 cup milk
- 3 tbsps. instant chocolate drink mix
- 2 tbsps. instant coffee granules
- 2 tbsps. honey
- 1 tsp. vanilla extract
- 14 to 16 ice cubes

Direction

1. Combine all the ingredients in a blender. Cover and process the mixture until smooth. Pour it into the chilled glasses to serve.

Nutrition Information

- Calories: 143 calories
- Total Carbohydrate: 30 g
- Cholesterol: 8 mg
- Total Fat: 3 g
- Fiber: 1 g
- Protein: 3 g
- Sodium: 72 mg

HAZELNUT COFFEE

Serving: 4

Preparation Time: 10 minutes

Cooking Time: 15 minutes

Ingredients

- 4 cups brewed coffee
- 1/4 cup hazelnut flavoring syrup
- 1 tbsp. sugar
- 1/8 tsp. ground cinnamon
- 1/4 cup heavy whipping cream
- 1 tbsp. Nutella

Direction

1. Then, combine the heat with cinnamon, sugar, flavoring syrup, and coffee in a big saucepan. Pour the coffee mixture into four mugs.
2. Beat Nutella and cream till thick in a small bowl. Gently top on the drinks, then serve immediately.

Nutrition Information

- Calories: 129 calories
- Total Carbohydrate: 16 g
- Cholesterol: 20 mg
- Total Fat: 7 g
- Fiber: 0 g
- Protein: 1 g
- Sodium: 12 mg

HAZELNUT MOCHA SMOOTHIE

Serving: 3

Preparation Time: 10 minutes

Cooking Time: 10 minutes

Ingredients

- 1 cup whole milk
- 1/2 cup Nutella
- 4 tsp. instant espresso powder
- Six ice cubes
- 2 cups vanilla ice cream
- Chocolate curls, optional

Direction

1. Combine espresso powder, Nutella, and milk in a blender. Cover and process till blended. Place in ice cubes, then cover; blend till smooth. Add ice cream, then cover; blend till soft. Transfer into chilled glasses. Immediately serve with chocolate curls as garnish if preferred.

Nutrition Information

- Calories: 474 calories
- Total Carbohydrate: 55 g
- Cholesterol: 47 mg
- Total Fat: 27 g
- Fiber: 2 g
- Protein: 9 g
- Sodium: 124 mg

ICED COFFEE

Serving: 2

Preparation Time: 2 minutes

Cooking Time: 2 minutes

Ingredients

- 1/2 cup warm water
- Two tips. instant coffee granules
- One tray of ice cubes
- 1/2 (5 oz.) can sweeten condensed milk
- 1/2 cup milk
- 1 tbsp. chocolate syrup

Direction

1. Combine instant coffee and water in a small bowl: mix chocolate syrup, sweetened condensed milk, milk, coffee mixture and ice cubes in a blender. Blend till smooth. Transfer into a glass. Serve.

Nutrition Information

- Calories: 171 calories;
- Total Carbohydrate: 28.4 g
- Cholesterol: 17 mg
- Total Fat: 4.4 g
- Protein: 5.1 g
- Sodium: 82 mg

CED COFFEE PERFECTION

Serving: 6

Preparation Time: 10 minutes

Cooking Time: 8h10 minutes

Ingredients

- 6 cups cold water
- 1 cup ground coffee beans
- 1 tbsp. vanilla extract (optional)
- 1 tbsp. ground cinnamon (optional)

Direction

1. In a resealable container or a jar, combine cinnamon, vanilla extract, coffee, and water, then stir well. Allow the coffee to stand for 8 hours overnight until the flavor intensifies (no need to refrigerate). Use a cheesecloth to strain the coffee into a separate container.

Nutrition Information

- Calories: 17 calories;
- Total Carbohydrate: 2.8 g
- Cholesterol: 0 mg
- Total Fat: 0 g
- Protein: 0.4 g
- Sodium: 15 mg

FRENCH ICED COFFEE

Serving: 15 servings (3-3/4 quarts).

Preparation Time: 10 minutes

Cooking Time: 10 minutes

Ingredients

- 5 cups hot brewed coffee
- 1-1/2 cups sugar
- 6 cups milk
- 3 cups heavy whipping cream
- 1/2 cup chocolate syrup

Direction

1. Whisk sugar and coffee in a big bowl till sugar is dissolved. Add in the leftover ingredients and stir. Divide into 1–1/2-quart portions and freeze in a freezer container overnight.
2. Refrigerate till slushy for 2-3 hours. Immediately serve.

Nutrition Information

- Calories: 328 calories
- Total Carbohydrate: 32 g
- Cholesterol: 75 mg
- Total Fat: 21 g
- Fiber: 0 g
- Protein: 4 g
- Sodium: 65 mg

FRENCH VANILLA CAPPUCCINO MIX

Serving: 1

Preparation Time: 20 minutes

Cooking Time: 20 minutes

Ingredients

- 1-1/2 cups instant hot cocoa mix
- One jar (8 oz.) powdered French Vanilla nondairy creamer
- 1 cup nonfat dry milk powder
- 1 cup confectioners' sugar
- 1/2 cup sugar
- 1/2 cup instant coffee granules
- EACH SERVING:
- 1 cup hot water
- Sweetened whipped cream and baking cocoa

Direction

1. Mix the first six ingredients in a big bowl. Keep in an airtight container for up to 2 months in a cool and dry place.
2. Yield 4 cups or 16 servings in total.
3. For cappuccino: In a coffee mug, put in 1/4 cup of mix and add 1 cup of hot water. Stir till combined. Place whipped cream on top and drizzle with baking soda.

Nutrition Information

- Calories: 186 calories
- Total Carbohydrate: 32 g
- Cholesterol: 1 mg
- Total Fat: 4 g
- Fiber: 1 g
- Protein: 3 g
- Sodium: 190 mg

FRENCH VANILLA MOCHA

Serving: 2

Preparation Time: 5 minutes

Cooking Time: 10 minutes

Ingredients

- 2 tbsps. instant coffee granules
- 2 tsp. chocolate syrup
- 1-1/2 cups 2% milk
- 1/2 cup refrigerated French vanilla coffee creamer

Direction

1. Add chocolate syrup and coffee granules into two mugs; put aside. Mix coffee creamer and milk in a small microwave-safe bowl. Uncovered, microwave for 1-2 minutes on high till hot. Pour into mugs and stir till coffee granules dissolve. Immediately serve.

Nutrition Information

- Calories: 274 calories
- Total Carbohydrate: 34 g
- Cholesterol: 14 mg
- Total Fat: 12 g
- Fiber: 0 g
- Protein: 7 g
- Sodium: 116 mg

CHOCOLATE COFFEE

Serving: 12

Preparation Time: 20 minutes

Cooking Time: 60 minutes

Ingredients

- 1 cup sugar
- 1 cup baking cocoa
- 1 cup boiling water
- 1 tsp. vanilla extract
- 1/4 tsp. salt

- 4 cups heavy whipping cream, whipped
- 8 cups hot strong brewed coffee or whole milk

Direction

1. Whisk water, cocoa, and sugar together in a big heavy saucepan till smooth. Over medium-low heat, cook and whisk for 35 minutes till soft peaks form when you lift the whisk, and the mixture looks like a hot fudge sauce. Take away from the heat. Mix in salt and vanilla. Pour into a bowl and leave in the fridge for at least 2 hours.
2. Beat the chocolate mixture. Mix in well 2 cups of whipped cream. Fold in the leftover whipped cream. Add about 1/2 cup of chocolate cream into 2/3 cup of milk or coffee for each Stir till blended.

Nutrition Information

- Calories: 362 calories
- Total Carbohydrate: 24 g
- Cholesterol: 109 mg
- Total Fat: 30 g
- Fiber: 1 g
- Protein: 3 g
- Sodium: 83 mg

CHOCOLATE-CARAMEL RUM COFFEE

Serving: 8

Preparation Time: 15 minutes

Cooking Time: 25 minutes

Ingredients

- Two cans (12 oz. each) evaporated milk
- 3/4 cup rum
- 1/2 cup chocolate syrup
- 1/2 cup caramel sundae syrup
- 1/4 cup packed brown sugar
- 4 cups hot brewed coffee
- 2 tbsps. coffee liqueur
- COFFEE WHIPPED CREAM:
- 1 cup heavy whipping cream

- 6 tbsps. confectioners' sugar
- 2 tbsps. coffee liqueur
- Coffee beans, optional

Direction

1. Combine brown sugar, syrups, rum, and milk in a large saucepan. Cook (don't boil) till hot over medium heat. Stir in liqueur and coffee.
2. In the meantime, beat cream in a small bowl until it thickens. Beat in confectioners' sugar till it forms stiff peaks. Fold in liqueur till combined.
3. Add the coffee mixture in mugs. Add coffee beans and a dollop of coffee whipped cream to garnish if preferred.

Nutrition Information

- Calories: 437 calories
- Total Carbohydrate: 50 g
- Cholesterol: 68 mg
- Total Fat: 16 g
- Fiber: 0 g
- Protein: 7 g
- Sodium: 166 mg

BANANA MILK COFFEE

Serving: 2

Preparation Time: 5 minutes

Cooking Time: 5 minutes

Ingredients

- 1 cup milk
- One very ripe banana
- 1 tbsp. simple syrup (optional)
- ice cubes
- 1 cup cold brew coffee

Direction

1. Blend simple syrup, banana, and milk for 1 minute until smooth.

2. Fill ice cubes into two 16-oz. glasses. Pour coffee among the glasses. Top with banana milk, then divides it between the glasses evenly.

Nutrition Information

- Calories: 133 calories;
- Total Carbohydrate: 23.9 g
- Cholesterol: 10 mg
- Total Fat: 2.6 g
- Protein: 4.8 g
- Sodium: 61 mg

BANANA MOCHA COOLER

Serving: 3

Preparation Time: 5 minutes

Cooking Time: 5 minutes

Ingredients

- 1 cup low-fat vanilla frozen yogurt
- 3/4 cup fat-free milk
- One medium ripe banana, sliced
- 1 tsp. instant coffee granules
- 1 cup ice cubes (7 to 8)

Direction

1. Combine all the ingredients in a blender. Cover and process the mixture for 45 to 60 seconds or until frothy. Pour it into the glasses to serve.

Nutrition Information

- Calories: 122 calories
- Total Carbohydrate: 24 g
- Cholesterol: 5 mg
- Total Fat: 1 g
- Fiber: 1 g
- Protein: 6 g
- Sodium: 72 mg

Serving: 2

Preparation Time: 10 minutes

Cooking Time: 15 minutes

Ingredients

- 1-1/2 tsp. butter
- 1/8 tsp. vanilla extract
- Dash each ground cinnamon, nutmeg, and cloves
- Four orange peel strips (1 to 3 inches)
- 3 oz. Cognac or brandy
- 2 cups strong brewed coffee
- 2 tbsps. packed brown sugar
- Cinnamon sticks and sweetened whipped cream, optional

Direction

1. Melt butter in a small skillet over medium-low heat. Add in orange peel, spices, and vanilla; stir. Take away from the heat; add Cognac. Take the pan back to the heat; ignite the Cognac mixture carefully.
2. Extinguish the flames by gradually pouring over with brewed coffee. Remove orange peel; add in brown sugar, and stir till blended. Transfer into mugs. Add whipped cream and cinnamon sticks (if desired), then serve immediately.

Nutrition Information

- Calories: 153 calories
- Total Carbohydrate: 14 g
- Cholesterol: 8 mg
- Total Fat: 3 g
- Fiber: 0 g
- Protein: 0 g
- Sodium: 27 mg

BUTTERSCOTCH COFFEE

Serving: 8 servings (2 quarts).

Preparation Time: 20 minutes

Cooking Time: 20 minutes

Ingredients

- 1 cup butterscotch chips, divided
- 8 cups hot brewed coffee
- 1/2 cup half-and-half cream
- 5 to 8 tbsps. sugar
- Whipped cream in a can

Direction

1. Melt 1/2 cup of cup butterscotch chips in a microwave till smooth. Make a small hole and insert a #4 round tip in the corner of a plastic bag or a pastry. Fill in melted chips. On a waxed paper-lined baking sheet, pipe eight garnishes, then store in the fridge for about 10 minutes till set.
2. Stir the leftover butterscotch chips and coffee till the chips melt in a big pitcher. Add in sugar and cream; stir. Transfer into mugs. Add a butterscotch garnish and whipped cream on top of each.

Nutrition Information

- Calories: 246 calories
- Total Carbohydrate: 30 g
- Cholesterol: 18 mg
- Total Fat: 13 g
- Fiber: 0 g
- Protein: 2 g
- Sodium: 50 mg

CAFE DULCE DE LECHE

Serving: 8

Preparation Time: 10 minutes

Cooking Time: 10 minutes

Ingredients

- 1/3 (11.5 oz.) jar dulce de leche
- 8 cups water
- 1/4 cup ground coffee beans

Direction

1. Put dulce de leche into a coffee maker's carafe—ground coffee after brewing with water. Allow the coffee to drip over dulce de leche. Stir till dissolved.

Nutrition Information

- Calories: 41 calories;
- Total Carbohydrate: 8.3 g
- Cholesterol: 2 mg
- Total Fat: 0.7 g
- Protein: 0.7 g
- Sodium: 35 mg

CAFE LATTE

Serving: 4

Preparation Time: 5 minutes

Cooking Time: 15 minutes

Ingredients

- 2 cups milk
- 1 1/3 cups hot freshly brewed dark roast espresso coffee

Direction

1. Heat milk over medium-low heat in a saucepan. Use a wire whisk to whisk briskly and create foam: brew espresso and transfer into 4 cups. Add in milk, use a spoon to hold back the foam. Add foam on top.

Nutrition Information

- Calories: 63 calories;
- Total Carbohydrate: 5.7 g
- Cholesterol: 10 mg

- Total Fat: 2.5 g
- Protein: 4.1 g
- Sodium: 61 mg

CAMPFIRE S'MORES FRAPPUCCINO®

Serving: 1

Preparation Time: 10 minutes

Cooking Time: 10 minutes

Ingredients

- 3/4 cup ice
- 1/2 cup milk
- 3 tbsps. marshmallow topping (such as Smucker's®)
- One-shot cold espresso
- 1/2 tbsp. Dutch-process cocoa powder
- 1/2 tbsp. white sugar
- 1/4 cup whipped cream
- 1/2 tbsp. graham cracker crumbs

Direction

1. In a blender, blend sugar, cocoa powder, espresso, marshmallow topping, milk, and ice until smooth. Transfer into a glass and place graham cracker crumbs and whipped on top.

Nutrition Information

- Calories: 199 calories;

- Total Carbohydrate: 31.6 g
- Cholesterol: 21 mg
- Total Fat: 6.5 g
- Protein: 5.4 g
- Sodium: 110 mg

CAMPFIRE S'MORES LATTE

Serving: 1

Preparation Time: 10 minutes

Cooking Time: 15 minutes

Ingredients

- One fluid oz. brewed espresso
- 3 tbsps. marshmallow ice cream topping (such as Smucker's®)
- 1 1/2 tsp. white sugar
- 1 1/2 tsp. cocoa powder
- 2/3 cup milk
- 1/4 cup whipped cream
- 1 tbsp. graham cracker crumbs

Direction

1. Add espresso in a mug; mix cocoa powder, sugar, and marshmallow topping until well blended.
2. Heat milk over medium-low heat for 3-5 minutes until boiling lightly in a saucepan. Take away from the heat. Use a whisk or a frothing wand to froth the milk. Over espresso mixture, pour frothed milk, then top with graham cracker crumbs and whipped cream.

Nutrition Information

- Calories: 231 calories;
- Total Carbohydrate: 35.6 g
- Cholesterol: 24 mg
- Total Fat: 7.6 g
- Protein: 6.9 g
- Sodium: 137 mg

CAPPUCCINO COOLER

Serving: 4

Preparation Time: 5 minutes

Cooking Time: 5 minutes

Ingredients

- 1 1/2 cups cold coffee
- 1 1/2 cups chocolate ice cream
- 1/4 cup chocolate syrup
- crushed ice
- 1 cup whipped cream

Direction

1. Combine chocolate syrup, ice cream and coffee in a blender, then blend till smooth. Over crushed ice, pour the mixture and use a dollop of whipped cream for garnish. Serve.

Nutrition Information

- Calories: 199 calories;
- Total Carbohydrate: 28 g
- Cholesterol: 28 mg
- Total Fat: 9 g
- Protein: 2.9 g
- Sodium: 72 mg

CAPPUCCINO PUNCH

Serving: about 1 gallon.

Preparation Time: 10 minutes

Cooking Time: 10 minutes

Ingredients

- 1/2 cup sugar
- 1/4 cup instant coffee granules
- 1 cup boiling water
- 2 quarts whole milk

- 1-quart vanilla ice cream softened
- 1-quart chocolate ice cream softened
- Grated chocolate, optional

Direction

1. Mix coffee and sugar; add in boiling water and stir till dissolves. Cover and store in the fridge till chilled.
2. Transfer the mixture into a 1-gal. Punch bowl right before mixing in milk. Stir in scoops of ice cream till melted. Drizzle with grated chocolate if preferred.

Nutrition Information

- Calories: 238 calories
- Total Carbohydrate: 29 g
- Cholesterol: 42 mg
- Total Fat: 11 g
- Fiber: 0 g
- Protein: 7 g
- Sodium: 112 mg

CAPPUCCINO SMOOTHIE

Serving: 3

Preparation Time: 5 minutes

Cooking Time: 5 minutes

Ingredients

- 1 cup (8 oz.) cappuccino or coffee yogurt

- 1/3 cup whole milk
- 3 tbsps. confectioners' sugar, optional
- 1 tbsp. chocolate syrup
- 1-1/2 cups ice cubes
- 1/2 cup miniature marshmallows, divided

Direction

1. Combine chocolate syrup, sugar (if preferred), milk and yogurt in a blender. Place in 1/4 cup of marshmallows and ice cubes. Cover and process till blended. Transfer into chilled glasses. Place the leftover marshmallows on top, then immediately serve.

Nutrition Information

- Calories: 166 calories
- Total Carbohydrate: 30 g
- Cholesterol: 11 mg
- Total Fat: 3 g
- Fiber: 0 g
- Protein: 5 g
- Sodium: 69 mg

CARAMEL-COCONUT ICED COFFEE

Serving: 1

Preparation Time: 5 minutes

Cooking Time: 5 minutes

Ingredients

- Six cubes ice cubes, or as needed
- 1/2 cup Gevalia® Cold Brew Concentrate - Caramel
- 1/2 cup sweetened coffee creamer
- 1 tbsp. coconut flavored syrup
- 1 tbsp. whipped topping (optional)
- 1 tsp. sweetened flaked coconut (optional)
- 2 tsp. caramel ice cream topping (optional)

Direction

1. Fill ice cubes in a large glass. Stir in coconut syrup, creamer and cold brew concentrate.

2. Add caramel syrup and coconut flakes, whipped topping as a garnish as preferred.

Nutrition Information

- Calories: 701 calories;
- Total Carbohydrate: 84.5 g
- Cholesterol: < 1 mg
- Total Fat: 30.1 g
- Protein: 0.3 g
- Sodium: 107 mg

CELTIC COFFEE

Serving: 1

Preparation Time: 10 minutes

Cooking Time: 13 minutes

Ingredients

- One egg white
- 1 tsp. lemon juice
- 1/2 tsp. stevia powder, or to taste
- 1/4 tsp. grated lemon zest, or to taste
- 3 tbsps. coarsely ground coffee beans
- 1 cup boiling water
- 2 tbsps. Scotch whiskey
- 2 tsp. honey

Direction

1. Use an electric mixer to beat egg white till it forms soft peaks in a bowl. Stir in lemon zest, stevia powder and lemon juice.
2. In a French press, add ground coffee and boiling water. Cover and allow to steep for 3-5 minutes.
3. In a glass, combine honey and Scotch, then add in coffee; mix well. Place lemon-flavored egg white on top.

Nutrition Information

- Calories: 148 calories;
- Total Carbohydrate: 16.4 g
- Cholesterol: 0 mg

- Total Fat: 0 g
- Protein: 4.2 g
- Sodium: 72 mg

CHILLED LEMON COFFEE

Serving: 3

Preparation Time: 10 minutes

Cooking Time: 10 minutes

Ingredients

- 2 cups strong brewed coffee (French or another dark roast), chilled
- 1 cup lemon sherbet, softened
- 2 tbsps. sugar
- 1 tbsp. lemon juice
- Lemon peel, optional

Direction

1. In a blender, add lemon juice, sugar, sherbet and coffee. Cover and process till smooth. Transfer into chilled glasses. Add lemon peel to garnish if preferred. Immediately serve.

Nutrition Information

- Calories: 105 calories
- Total Carbohydrate: 24 g
- Cholesterol: 3 mg
- Total Fat: 1 g
- Fiber: 0 g
- Protein: 1 g
- Sodium: 26 mg

CHOCOLATE CHAI COFFEE MIX

Serving: 40

Preparation Time: 5 minutes

Cooking Time: 5 minutes

Ingredients

- 2 cups white sugar
- 1/2 cup unsweetened cocoa powder
- 1 1/2 tsp. ground cinnamon
- 1/2 tsp. salt
- 1/2 tsp. ground ginger
- 1/4 tsp. ground white pepper
- 1/4 tsp. ground cloves
- 1/8 tsp. ground cardamom

Direction

1. Mix cardamon, cloves, pepper, ginger, salt, cinnamon, cocoa powder, and sugar in an airtight container. Seal and shake.

Nutrition Information

- Calories: 42 calories;
- Total Carbohydrate: 10.7 g
- Cholesterol: 0 mg
- Total Fat: 0.2 g
- Protein: 0.2 g
- Sodium: 29 mg

CHOCOLATE CHERRY CAPPUCCINO

Serving: 48 servings (6 cups cappuccino mix).

Preparation Time: 15 minutes

Cooking Time: 20 minutes

Ingredients

- 3 cups sugar

- 2 cups confectioners' sugar
- 1-1/3 cups powdered nondairy creamer
- 1-1/3 cups instant coffee granules
- 1 cup baking cocoa
- One envelope (.13 oz.) unsweetened cherry Kool-Aid mix
- EACH SERVING:
- 1 cup 2% milk
- 2 tbsps. miniature marshmallows

Direction

1. Combine the first six ingredients in a big airtight container. Keep for up to 2 months in a cool and dry place.
2. For cappuccino: In a mug, place 2 tbsp. Mix, then add in hot milk and stir till combined. Add marshmallow on top.

Nutrition Information

- Calories: 259 calories
- Total Carbohydrate: 37 g
- Cholesterol: 33 mg
- Total Fat: 9 g
- Fiber: 0 g
- Protein: 9 g
- Sodium: 124 mg

ABBEY'S WHITE CHOCOLATE LATTE

Serving: 2

Preparation Time: 5 minutes

Cooking Time: 10 minutes

Ingredients

- 1 1/2 cups milk
- 1 tbsp. heavy cream
- 1/8 tsp. vanilla extract
- 1 tbsp. white sugar
- 1/2 cup brewed espresso
- 1/4 cup white chocolate chips, chopped

Direction

1. In a saucepan, combine cream and milk. Whisk till frothy and hot over high heat. Take away from the heat; add sugar and vanilla, then stir. In a mug, whisk white chocolate chips and hot espresso until smooth. Pour half into another cup to make two. Add frothy hot milk on top and stir to blend with flavoring.

Nutrition Information

- Calories: 270 calories;
- Total Carbohydrate: 27.7 g
- Cholesterol: 30 mg
- Total Fat: 14.4 g
- Protein: 7.8 g
- Sodium: 110 mg

AFFOGATO WITH COLD-BREWED COFFEE

Serving: 2

Preparation Time: 5 minutes

Cooking Time: 12h5 minutes

Ingredients

- 2/3 cup medium-coarse ground coffee
- 3 cups cold water
- Two scoops of vanilla ice cream
- 2 tbsps. shaved dark chocolate

Direction

1. In a small bowl, whisk together cold water and ground coffee. Use plastic wrap to cover and put aside for 12 hours. Whisk, then use a funnel lined with a moistened paper towel to strain into a bowl.
2. Add ice cream scoops in 2 espresso or coffee cups. Pour 1/4-1/2 cup of cold coffee over each scoop of ice cream. Add shaved dark chocolate as garnish.

Nutrition Information

- Calories: 109 calories;
- Total Carbohydrate: 15.4 g
- Cholesterol: 9 mg
- Total Fat: 5.1 g
- Protein: 2.1 g
- Sodium: 46 mg

AFTER-DINNER MOCHA WHITE CHOCOLATE

Serving: 2

Preparation Time: 10 minutes

Cooking Time: 15 minutes

Ingredients

- 1-1/2 cups 2% milk
- 3 oz. white baking chocolate, chopped
- 2 tbsps. instant coffee granules
- 1 tsp. vanilla extract
- Optional toppings: whipped cream and baking cocoa

Direction

1. Heat milk in a small saucepan over medium heat till bubbles form around the pan's sides but don't bring to a boil.
2. In a blender, add in the leftover ingredients with hot milk. Cover and blend till frothy. Serve in mugs with whipped cream and cocoa on top if preferred.

Nutrition Information

- Calories: 342 calories

- Total Carbohydrate: 34 g
- Cholesterol: 23 mg
- Total Fat: 19 g
- Fiber: 0 g
- Protein: 9 g
- Sodium: 137 mg

ALMOND COFFEE CREAMER

Serving: 1-1/4 cups.

Preparation Time: 5 minutes

Cooking Time: 5 minutes

Ingredients

- 3/4 cup confectioners' sugar
- 3/4 cup powdered nondairy creamer
- 1 tsp. ground cinnamon
- 1 tsp. almond extract

Direction

1. Combine all the ingredients in a bowl, then mix well. Add to the coffee in place of sugar and nondairy creamer to serve. Keep in an airtight container.

Nutrition Information

- Calories: 71 calories
- Total Carbohydrate: 15 g
- Cholesterol: 0 mg
- Total Fat: 1 g
- Fiber: 0 g
- Protein: 0 g
- Sodium: 11 mg

CHOCOLATE-CHERRY COFFEE MIX

Serving: 1

Preparation Time: 15 minutes

Cooking Time: 20 minutes

Ingredients

- 3 cups sugar
- 2 cups confectioners' sugar
- 1-1/3 cups powdered nondairy creamer
- 1-1/3 cups instant coffee granules
- 1 cup baking cocoa
- One envelope (.13 oz.) unsweetened cherry soft drink mix
- 6 cups miniature marshmallows, divided
- 6 tsp. holiday sprinkles, divided
- ADDITIONAL INGREDIENT (for each serving):
- 1 cup hot whole milk

Direction

1. Combine the first six ingredients in an airtight container. Place for up to 2 months in a cool, dry place. Yield: 6 cups.
2. Add 1 cup mix into a 12-in—disposable decorating bag for a gift. Fold the bag's corners to the center, then roll the bag down. Use transparent tape to secure. Put the bag in another disposable decorating bag. Add 1 tsp of sprinkles and 1 cup of marshmallow on top. Gather, then twist the bag's top. Add ribbon and gift tag. Do the same to make five more gift bags. Yield: 6 gift bags with eight servings/1 cup per bag.
3. For coffee: Let two heaping tbsp. Mix dissolve in hot milk. Stir well, then add sprinkles and marshmallows on top.

Nutrition Information

- Calories: 131 calories
- Total Carbohydrate: 27 g
- Cholesterol: 4 mg
- Total Fat: 2 g
- Fiber: 0 g
- Protein: 2 g
- Sodium: 19 mg

CINNAMON MOCHA COFFEE

Serving: 4

Preparation Time: 5 minutes

Cooking Time: 15 minutes

Ingredients

- 1/3 cup ground coffee (not instant coffee granules)
- 3/4 tsp. ground cinnamon
- 1 cup 2% milk
- 2 to 3 tbsps. sugar
- 2 tbsps. baking cocoa
- 1 tsp. vanilla extract
- Four cinnamon sticks, optional
- Whipped cream, optional

Direction

1. Combine ground cinnamon and coffee in a coffeemaker basket. Follow the manufacturer's directions to prepare 4 cups of brewed coffee.
2. In the meantime, combine vanilla, cocoa, sugar and milk in a saucepan. Cook and occasionally stir over medium-low heat till a small bubble appears on the pan's sides, for 5-7 minutes. Don't bring to a boil. Into four coffee cups, pour hot milk mixture and add cinnamon-flavored coffee. Add whipped cream and cinnamon sticks to garnish if preferred.

Nutrition Information

- Calories: 77 calories
- Total Carbohydrate: 12 g
- Cholesterol: 8 mg
- Total Fat: 2 g
- Fiber: 1 g
- Protein: 3 g
- Sodium: 35 mg

CITRUS SPICED COFFEE

Serving: 9

Preparation Time: 15 minutes

Cooking Time: 15 minutes

Ingredients

- 3/4 cup ground coffee
- 1 tsp. grated lemon peel
- 1 cup water
- 3/4 cup packed brown sugar
- Three cinnamon sticks (3 inches)
- Two fresh orange slices
- 2 tbsps. unsweetened pineapple juice
- 1/2 tsp. vanilla extract

Direction

1. Add the coffee grounds to a coffeemaker's basket or filter—place in lemon peel. Follow the manufacturer's directions to prepare 9 cups of brewed coffee.
2. Combine vanilla, pineapple juice, orange slices, cinnamon sticks, brown sugar, and water in a small saucepan. Cook while stirring till the sugar dissolved over medium heat. Strain; remove oranges and cinnamon—transfer sugar mixture into mugs. Pour in coffee and stir.

Nutrition Information

- Calories: 90 calories
- Total Carbohydrate: 22 g
- Cholesterol: 0 mg
- Total Fat: 0 g
- Fiber: 0 g
- Protein: 1 g
- Sodium: 9 mg

COCONUT CARDAMOM ICED COFFEE

Serving: 3

Preparation Time: 7minutes

Cooking Time: 10 minutes

Ingredients

- 2 tsp. unsweetened coconut flakes
- One pinch ground cardamom
- 14 oz. Gevalia® Cold Brew Concentrate - House Blend
- 1/8 tsp. ground cardamom
- 1 (14 oz.) can light coconut milk
- 1 tsp. coconut extract, or to taste
- 1 tsp. white sugar, or to taste
- One tray of ice cubes

Direction

1. Over medium heat, add a pinch of cardamom and coconut flakes in a small pan. Constantly stir for 3-4 minutes till lightly brown. Take away from the heat.
2. Blend sweetener, coconut extract, coconut milk, 1/8 tsp cardamom and cold brew concentrate in a blender for 5-6 seconds till thoroughly mixed.
3. Fill ice in halfway of 3 big glasses. Pour coffee mixture into glasses and place shredded coconut on top.

Nutrition Information

- Calories: 287 calories;
- Total Carbohydrate: 7.9 g
- Cholesterol: 0 mg
- Total Fat: 28.7 g
- Protein: 2.8 g
- Sodium: 49 mg

COFFEE ALMOND FLOATS

Serving: 2

Preparation Time: 10 minutes

Cooking Time: 10 minutes

Ingredients

- 2 tbsps. instant coffee granules
- 1 tbsp. hot water
- 2 cups 2% milk
- 2 tbsps. brown sugar
- 1/8 tsp. almond extract
- 1 cup vanilla ice cream

Direction

1. Dissolve coffee granules in a minor pitcher in hot water. Add extract, brown sugar and milk. Into two chilled glasses, place a spoon of ice cream. Add the coffee mixture on top.

Nutrition Information

- Calories: 314 calories
- Total Carbohydrate: 42 g
- Cholesterol: 47 mg
- Total Fat: 12 g
- Fiber: 0 g
- Protein: 11 g
- Sodium: 181 mg

COFFEE HOUSE SLUSH

Serving: 5 quarts.

Preparation Time: 10 minutes

Cooking Time: 10 minutes

Ingredients

- 6 cups strong brewed coffee
- 2 cups sugar
- 2 quarts milk
- 1-quart half-and-half cream
- 4 tsp. vanilla extract
- Whipped cream, optional

Direction

1. Stir sugar and coffee in a 5-qt. Freezer container till sugar dissolves. Add in vanilla, cream and milk, then stir. Freeze overnight, covered.
2. Thaw in the fridge till slushy for 8-10 hours to serve. Scoop into glasses. Add whipped cream as garnish if preferred.

Nutrition Information

- Calories: 205 calories
- Total Carbohydrate: 26 g
- Cholesterol: 37 mg
- Total Fat: 8 g
- Fiber: 0 g
- Protein: 5 g
- Sodium: 73 mg

COFFEE LIQUEUR

Serving: 32

Preparation Time: 15 minutes

Cooking Time: 1h

Ingredients

- 4 cups white sugar
- 4 cups water
- 3/4 cup instant coffee granules
- 2 tbsps. vanilla extract
- 4 cups vodka

Direction

1. Combine water and sugar over medium heat in a 3-qt. Saucepan. Boil, then lower the heat; simmer for 10 minutes. Take away from the heat. Mix in instant coffee, let cool.
2. Once it's cooled, mix in vodka and vanilla extract. Cover tightly and keep in a cool dark place. Transfer into clean bottles.

Nutrition Information

- Calories: 169 calories;
- Total Carbohydrate: 25.5 g
- Cholesterol: 0 mg

- Total Fat: 0 g
- Protein: 0.1 g
- Sodium: < 1 mg

COFFEE PUNCH

Serving: 13 servings (2-1/2 quarts).

Preparation Time: 15 minutes

Cooking Time: 15 minutes

Ingredients

- 4 cups brewed vanilla-flavored coffee, cooled
- One can (12 oz.) evaporated milk
- 1/2 cup sugar
- 1/2 gallon vanilla ice cream, softened
- Ground cinnamon

Direction

1. Combine sugar, milk, and coffee in a big container till sugar dissolves—scoop ice cream into a punch bowl. Add coffee mixture over the top. Drizzle with cinnamon and immediately serve.

Nutrition Information

- Calories: 228 calories
- Total Carbohydrate: 30 g
- Cholesterol: 44 mg
- Total Fat: 11 g
- Fiber: 0 g
- Protein: 5 g
- Sodium: 91 mg

COFFEE SHAKE

Serving: 1

Preparation Time: 5 minutes

Cooking Time: 5 minutes

Ingredients

- 1 tsp. instant coffee granules
- 3/4 cup milk
- 1 tsp. vanilla extract
- 2 tsp. white sugar, or to taste
- Six ice cubes
- 2 tsp. chocolate syrup (optional)

Direction

1. Blend chocolate syrup, ice, sugar, vanilla extract, milk and instant coffee till smooth in a blender.

Nutrition Information

- Calories: 173 calories;
- Total Carbohydrate: 26 g
- Cholesterol: 15 mg
- Total Fat: 3.8 g

- Protein: 6.4 g
- Sodium: 89 mg

COFFEE SLUSH

Serving: 18

Preparation Time: 10 minutes

Cooking Time: 4h10 minutes

Ingredients

- 3 pints half-and-half cream
- 3 cups cold-brewed coffee
- 2 cups white sugar
- 2 tbsps. vanilla extract

Direction

1. Combine vanilla extract, sugar, coffee, and cream in a freezer-safe container. Cover the container and freeze for at least 3 hours till the mixture is solid.
2. Take the container from the freezer and defrost for 1 hour at room temperature. Use a fork to break the coffee mixture and form a slush-like consistency. Move to a big pitcher or a punch bowl.

Nutrition Information

- Calories: 212 calories;
- Total Carbohydrate: 26.4 g
- Cholesterol: 34 mg
- Total Fat: 10.7 g
- Protein: 2.8 g
- Sodium: 39 mg

COFFEE VIENNA

Serving: 1-1/2 cups mix (12 servings).

Preparation Time: 10 minutes

Cooking Time: 10 minutes

Ingredients

- 2/3 cup powdered nondairy creamer
- 2/3 cup sugar
- 1/2 cup instant coffee granules
- 1/2 tsp. ground cinnamon

Direction

1. Combine all the ingredients in an airtight container. Keep for up to 2 months in a cool, dry place.
2. For one serving: Let 2 tbsp. Mix dissolve in 1 cup of boiling water in a mug. Stir well.

Nutrition Information

- Calories: 74 calories
- Total Carbohydrate: 15 g
- Cholesterol: 0 mg
- Total Fat: 1 g
- Fiber: 0 g
- Protein: 0 g
- Sodium: 1 mg

COFFEE WITH CINNAMON AND CLOVES

Serving: 2

Preparation Time: 10 minutes

Cooking Time: 20 minutes

Ingredients

- 2 cups water
- 5 tsp. instant coffee granules
- 1/2 cinnamon stick (3 inches)
- Four whole cloves
- 5 tsp. sugar
- Whipped topping, optional

Direction

1. Combine cloves, cinnamon sticks, coffee granules and water in a small saucepan; boil. Take away from the heat. Allow standing with the cover on for 5-8 minutes. Strain and remove spices. Add in sugar and stir till dissolved. Pour into mugs. Add whipped topping (if preferred), then serve.

Nutrition Information

- Calories: 46 calories
- Total Carbohydrate: 11 g
- Cholesterol: 0 mg
- Total Fat: 0 g
- Fiber: 0 g
- Protein: 0 g
- Sodium: 1 mg

COLD BREWED ICED COFFEE

Serving: 4

Preparation Time: 5 minutes

Cooking Time: 8h13 minutes

Ingredients

- 1/2 cup coarsely ground coffee beans
- 4 cups water, divided
- 1 cup white sugar
- ice cubes

Direction

1. In a big measuring cup or a French press, place coffee beans and add in 2 cups of water. Allow the coffee to steep for 8 hours to overnight.
2. Combine sugar and the leftover 2 cups of water in a saucepan; boil. Simmer for 3-5 minutes till sugar dissolves. Add syrup into a container and move to the fridge.
3. Use a coffee filter in a fine-mesh strainer or a French press plunger to strain the coffee. Into a glass of ice, pour 1/2 cup of coffee and add simple syrup to sweeten.

Nutrition Information

- Calories: 199 calories;
- Total Carbohydrate: 51.2 g
- Cholesterol: 0 mg
- Total Fat: 0 g
- Protein: 0.3 g
- Sodium: 14 mg

COLD-BREWED COFFEE

Serving: 6

Preparation Time: 10 minutes

Cooking Time: 18h10 minutes

Ingredients

- 1/2 lb. coarsely ground coffee beans
- 4 1/2 cups cold water
- cheesecloth
- coffee filters

Direction

1. In an enormous container, add coffee grounds and gradually pour water over them.
2. Use plastic wrap to cover and let steep for 18-24 hours at room temperature.
3. Line several layers of cheesecloth on a filter, then position atop a pitcher—strain coffee into the pitcher through the cheesecloth. Remove the grounds. Strain coffee through coffee filters again for a more transparent brew. Keep in the fridge.

Nutrition Information

- Calories: 8 calories;
- Total Carbohydrate: 1.5 g
- Cholesterol: 0 mg
- Total Fat: 0 g
- Protein: 0.4 g
- Sodium: 13 mg

COMFORT IN A CUP

Serving: 1

Preparation Time: 5 minutes

Cooking Time: 5 minutes

Ingredients

- 3/4 cup hot coffee
- 1/2 cup milk

- Two fluid oz. Irish cream liqueur (such as Baileys®)
- 2 tbsps. instant hot chocolate mix
- One fluid oz. vodka

Direction

1. In a mug, whisk vodka, hot chocolate mix, Irish cream liqueur, milk and hot coffee together till hot chocolate dissolves.

Nutrition Information

- Calories: 411 calories;
- Total Carbohydrate: 46.6 g
- Cholesterol: 10 mg
- Total Fat: 3.3 g
- Protein: 5.3 g
- Sodium: 139 mg

COMFORTING COFFEE MILK

Serving: 6

Preparation Time: 5 minutes

Cooking Time: 20 minutes

Ingredients

- 4 cups whole milk
- 1-1/3 cups strong brewed coffee
- 1/2 cup maple syrup
- 2 tbsps. molasses
- 2 tsp. baking cocoa
- WHIPPED CREAM:
- 1 cup heavy whipping cream
- 1 tbsp. maple syrup
- 1 tsp. vanilla extract
- Additional baking cocoa

Direction

1. Combine the first five ingredients in a big saucepan over medium heat to simmer while occasionally stirring (don't bring to a boil).

2. In the meantime, beat cream in a small bowl until it thickens. Beat in vanilla and maple syrup till it forms soft peaks. Serve with a dust of additional cocoa and coffee milk.

Nutrition Information

- Calories: 338 calories
- Total Carbohydrate: 34 g
- Cholesterol: 71 mg
- Total Fat: 20 g
- Fiber: 0 g
- Protein: 6 g
- Sodium: 91 mg

COOL COFFEE REFRESHER

Serving: 2

Preparation Time: 10 minutes

Cooking Time: 10 minutes

Ingredients

- 1 cup strong brewed coffee, chilled
- 1/4 tsp. vanilla extract
- 1/2 cup vanilla yogurt
- 3 tbsps. sugar
- 1 to 1-1/2 cups ice cubes

Direction

1. Combine sugar, yogurt, vanilla, and coffee in a blender. Cover, blend till smooth. Place in ice, then cover; process till mixed. Transfer into chilled glasses and immediately serve.

Nutrition Information

- Calories: 126 calories
- Total Carbohydrate: 27 g
- Cholesterol: 3 mg
- Total Fat: 1 g
- Fiber: 0 g
- Protein: 3 g
- Sodium: 41 mg

CREAMY CARAMEL MOCHA

Serving: 6

Preparation Time: 10 minutes

Cooking Time: 20 minutes

Ingredients

- 1/2 cup heavy whipping cream
- 1 tbsp. confectioners' sugar
- 1 tsp. vanilla extract, divided
- 1/4 cup Dutch-processed cocoa
- 1-1/2 cups half-and-half cream
- 4 cups hot strong brewed coffee
- 1/2 cup caramel flavoring syrup
- Butterscotch-caramel ice cream topping

Direction

1. Beat whipping cream in a small bowl till it starts to thicken. Beat 1/2 tsp of vanilla and confectioners' sugar until it forms stiff peaks.
2. Whisk half-and-half cream and cocoa over medium heat in a big saucepan till smooth. Heat till bubbles form around the pan's sides. Whisk in the leftover vanilla, caramel syrup and coffee. Place whipped cream on top and sprinkle with butterscotch topping.
3. To prepare using a slow cooker: Follow as directed to prepare the whipped cream. Whisk the leftover vanilla, caramel syrup, coffee, half-and-half and cocoa together in a 3-qt—slow cooker. Cover then cook till heat through, for 2-3 hours. As directed, serve.

Nutrition Information

- Calories: 220 calories
- Total Carbohydrate: 19 g
- Cholesterol: 57 mg
- Total Fat: 14 g
- Fiber: 1 g
- Protein: 3 g
- Sodium: 38 mg

CREAMY COFFEE MIX

Serving: 5 servings (1 cup mix).

Preparation Time: 10 minutes

Cooking Time: 10 minutes

Ingredients

- 7 tbsps. instant coffee granules
- 1/4 cup powdered nondairy creamer
- 3 tbsps. sugar
- 3 tbsps. nonfat dry milk powder
- 1 tsp. ground cinnamon
- ADDITIONAL INGREDIENTS (for each batch):
- 1 cup boiling water
- Cinnamon sticks, optional

Direction

1. Combine the first five ingredients in a small bowl; mix well. Keep for up to 2 months in a cool, dry place in an airtight container. Yield: 5 batches or about 1 cup total.
2. For coffee: During storage, the contents of the mix may settle. Before measuring, stir the mixture and add 3 tbsp. Of coffee mix in a mug. Add in and mix boiling water till blended. Add a cinnamon stick and serve if preferred.

Nutrition Information

- Calories: 78 calories
- Total Carbohydrate: 16 g
- Cholesterol: 1 mg
- Total Fat: 1 g
- Fiber: 0 g
- Protein: 2 g
- Sodium: 33 mg

CREAMY IRISH COFFEE

Serving: 4

Preparation Time: 10 minutes

Cooking Time: 10 minutes

Ingredients

- 3 cups hot strong brewed coffee
- 4 oz. Irish cream liqueur
- Sweetened whipped cream, optional
- Chocolate shavings, optional

Direction

1. Add liqueur and coffee into four mugs, then stir. Add chocolate shaving and whipped cream on top if preferred.

Nutrition Information

- Calories: 118 calories
- Total Carbohydrate: 8 g
- Cholesterol: 0 mg
- Total Fat: 4 g
- Fiber: 0 g
- Protein: 0 g
- Sodium: 1 mg

CREAMY VANILLA COFFEE

Serving: 3

Preparation Time: 10 minutes

Cooking Time: 10 minutes

Ingredients

- 1/3 cup ground coffee
- 1 cup water
- 1/4 cup sugar
- 2 tbsps. instant vanilla pudding mix
- 2-1/2 cups 2% milk

Direction

1. Add ground coffee in a drip coffeemaker's coffee filter. Add water and follow the manufacturer's directions to brew.

2. Combine dry pudding mix and sugar in a small bowl. Add in and stir coffee and milk. Let chill till serving.

Nutrition Information

- Calories: 224 calories
- Total Carbohydrate: 35 g
- Cholesterol: 20 mg
- Total Fat: 7 g
- Fiber: 0 g
- Protein: 7 g
- Sodium: 204 mg

CREOLE COFFEE

Serving: 1

Preparation Time: 5 minutes

Cooking Time: 5 minutes

Ingredients

- 1 cup hot brewed coffee with chicory
- 1 tbsp. molasses
- 1 tbsp. half and half, or more to taste

Direction

1. Add coffee in a big mug. Add in half-and-half cream and molasses; stir till smooth.

Nutrition Information

- Calories: 85 calories;
- Total Carbohydrate: 17.4 g
- Cholesterol: 6 mg
- Total Fat: 1.7 g
- Protein: 0.7 g
- Sodium: 30 mg

EASY BREVE

Serving: 1

Preparation Time: 5 minutes

Cooking Time: 10 minutes

Ingredients

- 1/2 cup half-and-half cream
- 1/3 cup hot brewed Easy Espresso

Direction

1. Add cream in a 1-cup microwave-safe measuring cup. Uncover and microwave for 1 minute on high till tiny bubbles form around the cup's edge and milk is hot.
2. Put in the cup a metal whisk. Loosely keep the whisk handle between palms and rub hands back and forth quickly to whisk vigorously. When foam forms, transfer it to a small measuring cup. Keep whisking till foam fill 1/3 of the cup. Put aside.
3. Add Easy Espresso in a cup. Add in the leftover hot cream. Top with foam, then immediately serve.

Nutrition Information

- Calories: 161 calories
- Total Carbohydrate: 4 g
- Cholesterol: 60 mg
- Total Fat: 12 g
- Fiber: 0 g
- Protein: 4 g
- Sodium: 61 mg

EASY CAPPUCCINO

Serving: 1

Preparation Time: 5 minutes

Cooking Time: 10 minutes

Ingredients

- 1/2 cup milk
- 1/3 cup hot brewed Easy Espresso

Direction

1. Pour milk in a 1-cup microwave-safe measuring cup. Uncover, microwave for 1 minute on high till milk forms tiny bubbles around the cup's edge, and it's hot.
2. Put a metal whisk in a cup. Loosely hold the handle between palms and rub hands back and forth quickly to whisk vigorously. Discard foam when it forms into a small measuring cup. Keep whisking till 1/3 cup is filled with foam. Put aside.
3. Add Easy Espresso in a mug; pour in the leftover hot milk. Top with foam and immediately serve.

Nutrition Information

- Calories: 76 calories
- Total Carbohydrate: 6 g
- Cholesterol: 17 mg
- Total Fat: 4 g
- Fiber: 0 g
- Protein: 4 g
- Sodium: 61 mg

EASY ESPRESSO

Serving: 4

Preparation Time: 5 minutes

Cooking Time: 10 minutes

Ingredients

- 1/2 cup ground coffee (French or other dark roasts)
- 1-1/2 cups cold water
- Lemon twists, optional

Direction

1. Put the ground coffee on a drip coffeemaker's filter, then water. Follow the manufacturer's instructions to brew. Immediately serve with lemon twists (if preferred) in espresso cups.

Nutrition Information

- Calories: 7 calories
- Total Carbohydrate: 1 g
- Cholesterol: 0 mg

- Total Fat: 0 g
- Fiber: 0 g
- Protein: 0 g
- Sodium: 7 mg

EASY FRENCH ICED COFFEE

Serving: 10

Preparation Time: 10 minutes

Cooking Time: 10 minutes

Ingredients

- 3 cups strong brewed hot coffee
- 1-1/2 cups sugar
- 4 cups 2% milk
- 2 cups half-and-half cream
- 2 tsp. vanilla extract

Direction

1. Whisk sugar and coffee in a big bowl till sugar dissolves. Add vanilla, cream and milk; stir. Freeze for 8 hours or overnight in a 3-qt. Freezer container. 4 hours before serving move to the fridge. Stir till slushy, then immediately serve.

Nutrition Information

- Calories: 231 calories
- Total Carbohydrate: 36 g
- Cholesterol: 31 mg
- Total Fat: 7 g
- Fiber: 0 g
- Protein: 5 g
- Sodium: 73 mg

EASY ICED COFFEE

Serving: 1

Preparation Time: 5 minutes

Cooking Time: 10 minutes

Ingredients

- 2 tsp. instant coffee granules
- 1 tsp. sugar
- 3 tbsps. warm water
- Six fluid oz. cold milk

Direction

1. Combine warm water, sugar and instant coffee in a sealable jar.
2. Cover and shake the jar till foamy.
3. Transfer into a glass filled with ice. Pour milk into the glass and, If necessary, adjust to taste.

Nutrition Information

- Calories: 116 calories;
- Total Carbohydrate: 14.2 g
- Cholesterol: 15 mg
- Total Fat: 3.6 g
- Protein: 6.5 g
- Sodium: 78 mg

EASY PUMPKIN SPICE LATTE

Serving: 1

Preparation Time: 5 minutes

Cooking Time: 5 minutes

Ingredients

- 2 tbsps. half-and-half
- 2 tsp. white sugar, or to taste
- 1/4 tsp. pumpkin pie spice
- 1 cup coffee
- 1 tbsp. whipped cream topping, or to taste (optional)

Direction

1. Combine pumpkin pie spice, sugar, and half-and-half in a coffee mug. Add coffee into mugs, then stir to blend.
2. Heat in microwave for about 15 seconds till hot. Add whipped cream on top.

Nutrition Information

- Calories: 88 calories;
- Total Carbohydrate: 10.8 g
- Cholesterol: 11 mg
- Total Fat: 4.6 g
- Protein: 1.2 g
- Sodium: 18 mg

EASY COLD BREW COFFEE

Serving: 4

Preparation Time: 10 minutes

Cooking Time: 20h10 minutes

Ingredients

- 4 cups water
- 1/2 cup dark roast ground coffee (such as Folgers®)
- 2 cups 2% milk

- 1/4 cup white sugar
- 4 cups ice

Direction

1. In a French press, combine ground coffee and water the stir to make sure coffee and water are mixed evenly. Slowly push the plunger halfway down. Allow the coffee to steep for 20-24 hours at room temperature.
2. In a pitcher, combine sugar and milk till sugar dissolves. Push the French press plunger down. Add coffee on top of the cream. Pour coffee mixture into four glasses; place ice on top.

Nutrition Information

- Calories: 115 calories;
- Total Carbohydrate: 19.4 g
- Cholesterol: 10 mg
- Total Fat: 2.4 g
- Protein: 4.3 g
- Sodium: 70 mg

EATING WELL FROZEN MOCHACCINO

Serving: 2

Preparation Time: 10 minutes

Cooking Time: 4h10 minutes

Ingredients

- 1 cup double-strength brewed coffee or espresso (see Tip)
- 1 cup low-fat milk
- 2 tbsps. unsweetened natural cocoa powder (not Dutch-process), plus more for sprinkling
- 2-3tbsps. pure maple syrup
- ⅛ tsp. vanilla extract
- 1-2 ice cubes, if needed

Direction

1. Freeze the coffee in an ice cube tray for at least 4 hours or overnight until firm.
2. In a blender, mix maple syrup to taste, frozen coffee cubes, vanilla, milk and cocoa and then pulse, adding plain ice cubes if you prefer it thicker or a little water, until the resulting mixture is smooth.

3. To make it thinner. Split into two glasses, dust with a bit of cocoa powder if you want to, and then serve right away.

Nutrition Information

- Calories: 127 calories;
- Total Carbohydrate: 24 g
- Cholesterol: 6 mg
- Total Fat: 2 g
- Fiber: 2 g
- Protein: 5 g
- Sodium: 74 mg
- Sugar: 20 g
- Saturated Fat: 1 g

ICED COFFEE SYRUP

Serving: 4

Preparation Time: 10 minutes

Cooking Time: 10 minutes

Ingredients

- 1/4 cup instant coffee granules
- 2 cups hot water
- 1 (14 oz.) can sweeten condensed milk

Direction

1. Combine hot water with the instant coffee granules and stir till they dissolve.
2. Add in the condensed milk and stir. Keep in a jar or an airtight container. Place in the fridge till ready to use.

Nutrition Information

- Calories: 321 calories;
- Total Carbohydrate: 54.3 g
- Cholesterol: 33 mg
- Total Fat: 8.5 g
- Protein: 8.1 g
- Sodium: 129 mg

ICED HORCHATA COFFEE

Serving: 4

Preparation Time: 15 minutes

Cooking Time: 15 minutes

Ingredients

- 1 cup uncooked white rice
- 2 cups water
- 1/2 cup raw almonds
- 16 oz. Gevalia® Cold Brew Concentrate - House Blend
- 1 tbsp. blue agave nectar
- One tray of ice cubes
- Four cinnamon sticks (optional)

Direction

1. In a blender, mix almonds, water and rice, then blend for 2 minutes till the mixture is well combined. The mixture should be coarse.
2. Through a cheesecloth or a fine sieve, strain mixture into a pitcher; remove solids. Stir in blue agave and cold brew concentrate.
3. Serve over ice and use cinnamon sticks to garnish if preferred.

Nutrition Information

- Calories: 311 calories;
- Total Carbohydrate: 50.7 g
- Cholesterol: 0 mg
- Total Fat: 9.3 g
- Protein: 7.1 g
- Sodium: 31 mg

CED MOCHA FRAPPE

Serving: 2

Preparation Time: 8m

Cooking Time: 3h8m

Ingredients

- 1 1/2 cups cold coffee
- 2 cups whole milk
- 1/4 cup chocolate syrup
- 1/4 cup white sugar
- 1 tbsp. whipped cream (optional)

Direction

1. Add coffee into an ice cube tray. Freeze for 3-4 hours till solid.
2. In a blender, place frozen coffee cubes, then add sugar, chocolate syrup and milk. Blend till smooth.
3. In 2 glasses, pour the coffee mixture and add whipped cream on top.

Nutrition Information

- Calories: 353 calories;
- Total Carbohydrate: 60.6 g
- Cholesterol: 26 mg
- Total Fat: 8.7 g
- Protein: 8.9 g
- Sodium: 130 mg

EGGNOG COFFEE

Serving: 4 servings, about 1 cup each

Preparation Time: 10 minutes

Cooking Time: 10 minutes

Ingredients

- 1/4 cup ground MAXWELL HOUSE Coffee, any variety
- 1/4 tsp. ground nutmeg

- 2 Tbsp. sugar
- 2-1/2 cups cold water
- 1 cup eggnog, warmed
- 1/2 cup thawed COOL WHIP Whipped Topping

Direction

1. Place nutmeg and coffee in a filter in the coffee maker's brew basket. Add sugar to the empty coffee maker's pot.
2. Pour water in the coffee maker, then brew. Stir in eggnog once it completes brewing.
3. Transfer into 4 cups and add COOL WHIP on top.

Nutrition Information

- Calories: 110
- Total Carbohydrate: 16 g
- Cholesterol: 40 mg
- Total Fat: 4.5 g
- Fiber: 1 g
- Protein: 3 g
- Sodium: 45 mg
- Sugar: 16 g
- Saturated Fat: 3.5 g

EGGNOG LATTE

Serving: 1

Preparation Time: 4 minutes

Cooking Time: 5 minutes

Ingredients

- 1/3 cup 2% milk
- 2/3 cup eggnog
- 1 (1.5 fluid oz.) jigger brewed espresso
- One pinch of ground nutmeg

Direction

1. In a steaming pitcher, add eggnog and milk, then heat to between 145-165°F or 65-70°C with the steaming wand. Add foam on top. Brew espresso shot; pour into the mug. Add eggnog and

steamed milk into the cup; hold back the foam with a spoon. Drizzle on top of the foam with nutmeg.

Nutrition Information

- Calories: 275 calories;
- Total Carbohydrate: 27.2 g
- Cholesterol: 106 mg
- Total Fat: 14.7 g
- Protein: 9.2 g
- Sodium: 131 mg

FLAVORED CAPPUCCINO MIX

Serving: 15

Preparation Time: 10 minutes

Cooking Time: 10 minutes

Ingredients

- 1/3 cup dry milk powder
- 2/3 cup white sugar
- 2/3 cup powdered non-dairy creamer
- 1/3 cup instant coffee granules

Direction

1. Combine instant coffee granules, coffee creamer, sugar and powdered milk in a mixing bowl. Keep in an airtight container.
2. Add 2-3 tsp of mix into 1 cup of hot water and stir to prepare the beverage.

Nutrition Information

- Calories: 70 calories;
- Total Carbohydrate: 13.1 g
- Cholesterol: < 1 mg
- Total Fat: 1.5 g
- Protein: 1.3 g
- Sodium: 22 mg

FLAVORED LATTE

Serving: 1

Preparation Time: 4 minutes

Cooking Time: 5 minutes

Ingredients

- 1 1/4 cups 2% milk
- 2 tbsps. any flavor of flavored syrup
- 1 (1.5 fluid oz.) jigger brewed espresso

Direction

1. In a steaming pitcher, add milk, using a steaming wand, heat to 145°F - 165°F (65°C – 70°C). In a large coffee mug, put the flavored syrup. Brew espresso and pour in the cup. Using a spoon to keep the foam, add the steamed milk to the cup. Scoop the foam off the top.

Nutrition Information

- Calories: 261 calories;
- Total Carbohydrate: 41.3 g
- Cholesterol: 24 mg
- Total Fat: 6.1 g
- Protein: 10.1 g
- Sodium: 142 mg

FRAPPE MOCHA

Serving: 2

Preparation Time: 5 minutes

Cooking Time: 5 minutes

Ingredients

- 1 tsp. instant coffee granules
- 1/4 cup boiling water
- 1 cup fat-free milk
- 4-1/2 tsp. chocolate syrup
- 1/2 cup crushed ice

- Whipped topping and additional chocolate syrup, optional

Direction

1. Let coffee granules dissolve in water in a small bowl. Add into an ice cube tray and freeze.
2. Combine coffee ice cubes, chocolate syrup and milk in a blender—Mix with the cover until smooth. Put crushed ice in and blend. Transfer into chilled glasses and immediately serve. Add chocolate and whipped topping as garnish if preferred.

Nutrition Information

- Calories: 80 calories
- Total Carbohydrate: 15 g
- Cholesterol: 2 mg
- Total Fat: 0 g
- Fiber: 0 g
- Protein: 5 g
- Sodium: 61 mg

SWEET VIETNAMESE COFFEE

Serving: 1

Preparation Time: 5 minutes

Cooking Time: 10 minutes

Ingredients

- 2 tbsps. sweetened condensed milk
- 3 1/2 tsp. ground coffee with chicory
- boiling water

Direction

1. Into a coffee cup, add condensed milk.
2. Unscrew the Vietnamese coffee filter's top screen. Put in coffee; tightly screw screen back. Place filter over the cup.
3. Fill boiling water in 1/4 of the filter. Wait about 30 seconds till it passes through the filter. Slightly loosen the top screen. Fill boiling water in the filter. Put the lid on to cover, then wait about 5 minutes till it passes through the filter. Discard the filter.

Nutrition Information

- Calories: 125 calories;
- Total Carbohydrate: 21.2 g
- Cholesterol: 13 mg
- Total Fat: 3.3 g
- Protein: 3.2 g
- Sodium: 62 mg

TAN AND SWEET KETO COFFEE

Serving: 1

Preparation Time: 5 minutes

Cooking Time: 5 minutes

Ingredients

- Ten fluid oz. freshly brewed coffee
- 1/3 cup heavy cream
- 2 tbsps. grass-fed butter softened
- 1 tbsp. xylitol
- 1/2 tbsp. medium-chain triglyceride (MCT) oil, or to taste
- 1 tsp. vanilla extract

Direction

1. Combine vanilla extract, MCT oil, xylitol, butter, cream, and hot coffee in a travel mug. Secure the lid, then shake till combined.

Nutrition Information

- Calories: 580 calories;
- Total Carbohydrate: 14.8 g
- Cholesterol: 170 mg
- Total Fat: 59.5 g
- Protein: 2.2 g
- Sodium: 200 mg

TEMBLEQUE LATTE

Serving: 1

Preparation Time: 5 minutes

Cooking Time: 10 minutes

Ingredients

- One-shot brewed espresso
- 1 (1.5 fluid oz.) jigger coconut-flavored syrup (such as DaVinci®)
- 1/2 cup milk
- One pinch of ground cinnamon

Direction

1. In a mug, mix coconut syrup with espresso. Pour the milk into a saucepan and heat it at medium to low heat for around 5 minutes until it starts to boil. In the espresso mixture, stir the warm milk. Finish off by sprinkling cinnamon into the latte.

Nutrition Information

- Calories: 215 calories;
- Total Carbohydrate: 44.3 g
- Cholesterol: 10 mg
- Total Fat: 2.5 g
- Protein: 4.1 g
- Sodium: 69 mg

FRUGAL SUMMER COFFEE

Serving: 2

Preparation Time: 5 minutes

Cooking Time: 5 minutes

Ingredients

- 2 cups skim milk
- 2 cups coffee, at room temperature
- 2 tbsps. white sugar
- 1 tsp. vanilla extract

- 1/2 tsp. almond extract
- ice cubes

Direction

1. In a 1-qt. Container combines almond extract, vanilla extract, sugar, coffee, and skim milk. Store in the fridge till Pour over ice.

Nutrition Information

- Calories: 143 calories;
- Total Carbohydrate: 24.9 g
- Cholesterol: 5 mg
- Total Fat: 0.3 g
- Protein: 8.5 g
- Sodium: 112 mg

GINGERBREAD COFFEE

Serving: 6

Preparation Time: 20 minutes

Cooking Time: 30 minutes

Ingredients

- 1/2 cup molasses

- 1/4 cup brown sugar
- 1/2 tsp. baking soda
- 1 tsp. ground ginger
- 3/4 tsp. ground cinnamon
- 6 cups hot brewed coffee
- 1 cup half-and-half cream
- 1 tsp. ground cloves
- 1 1/2 cups sweetened whipped cream

Direction

1. Combine cinnamon, ginger, baking soda, brown sugar and molasses in a small bowl till blended well. Cover and place in the fridge for at least 10 minutes.
2. To each cup, add about 1/4 cup of coffee. Mix in about a tbsp. Of spice mixture till dissolves. Within an in. of the top, fill in coffee, then mix in half-and-half to taste. Add a light sprinkle of cloves and whipped cream to garnish.

Nutrition Information

- Calories: 198 calories;
- Total Carbohydrate: 30.6 g
- Cholesterol: 26 mg
- Total Fat: 8.1 g
- Protein: 2 g
- Sodium: 158 mg

HOMEMADE CINNAMON MOCHA COFFEE

Serving: 6

Preparation Time: 20 minutes

Cooking Time: 20 minutes

Ingredients

- 1/2 cup ground dark roast coffee
- 1 tbsp. ground cinnamon
- 1/4 tsp. ground nutmeg
- 5 cups water
- 1 cup 2% milk
- 1/3 cup chocolate syrup

- 1/4 cup packed brown sugar
- 1 tsp. vanilla extract
- Whipped cream, optional

Direction

1. Combine nutmeg, cinnamon and coffee grounds in a small bowl. Add water and follow to manufacturer's directions to brew. Pour into a drip coffeemaker's coffee filter.
2. Combine brown sugar, chocolate syrup and milk in a big saucepan. Cook while occasionally stirring over low heat till sugar dissolves. Add in brewed coffee and vanilla; stir. Transfer into mugs; add whipped cream to garnish if preferred.

Nutrition Information

- Calories: 126 calories
- Total Carbohydrate: 25 g
- Cholesterol: 6 mg
- Total Fat: 2 g
- Fiber: 1 g
- Protein: 3 g
- Sodium: 34 mg

HOMEMADE COFFEE MIX

Serving: 8

Preparation Time: 10 minutes

Cooking Time: 15 minutes

Ingredients

- BASIC COFFEE MIX:
- 1/3 cup sugar
- 1/4 cup nondairy creamer
- 1/4 cup instant coffee granules
- ADDITIONAL INGREDIENTS FOR MOCHA COFFEE:
- 2 tsp. baking cocoa
- FOR ORANGE CAPPUCCINO COFFEE:
- Six orange Lifesavers, finely crushed
- FOR VIENNESE COFFEE:
- 1/2 tsp. ground cinnamon

1. Combine and store coffee mix ingredients in an airtight container.
2. For preparation: Combine 8 cups of boiling water with the mix or use 2 tbsp. Mix per cup. Stir till dissolved.
3. Before adding water, add the additional ingredient to the basic mix for any flavored coffees.

Nutrition Information

- Calories: 50 calories
- Total Carbohydrate: 10 g
- Cholesterol: 0 mg
- Total Fat: 1 g
- Fiber: 0 g
- Protein: 0 g
- Sodium: 1 mg

HONEY SPICED LATTE

Serving: 4

Preparation Time: 15 minutes

Cooking Time: 20 minutes

Ingredients

- 1/2 cup ground coffee
- 1-1/2 cups cold water
- 1-1/3 cups milk
- 2 tbsps. honey
- 2 tbsps. molasses
- 4 tsp. sugar
- 1/4 tsp. ground ginger
- 1/4tsp. ground cinnamon
- 1/8 tsp. ground nutmeg
- 1/8 tsp. ground cloves
- Whipped cream, optional

Direction

1. Put ground coffee in a drip coffeemaker's filter. Add water, then follow the manufacturer's instructions to brew.

2. Mix spices, sugar, molasses, honey and milk in a small saucepan. Cook and stir till steaming over medium heat. Take away from the heat. Pour into a blender; cover and blend till foamy for 15 seconds.

3. Pour into four mugs, then add the coffee. Use whipped cream for garnish if preferred.

Nutrition Information

- Calories: 134 calories
- Total Carbohydrate: 26 g
- Cholesterol: 8 mg
- Total Fat: 3 g
- Fiber: 0 g
- Protein: 3 g
- Sodium: 44 mg

HOT BUTTERED COFFEE

Serving: 20 servings (1-1/4 cups mix).

Preparation Time: 15 minutes

Cooking Time: 15 minutes

Ingredients

- 1 cup packed brown sugar
- 1/4 cup butter, softened
- 1 tsp. vanilla extract
- 1/2 tsp. ground cinnamon
- 1/4 tsp. ground nutmeg
- 1/4 tsp. ground allspice
- 1/8 tsp. ground cloves
- EACH SERVING:
- 1 cup hot brewed coffee (French or another dark roast)
- Cinnamon sticks and whipped cream, optional

Direction

1. Combine the first seven ingredients till blended in a small bowl. Keep up to 2 weeks in an airtight container in the fridge.

2. For hot buttered coffee preparing: In a mug, add 1 tbsp. Of spice mixture, then mix in the coffee. Serve with whipped cream and cinnamon stick if preferred.

- Calories: 67 calories
- Total Carbohydrate: 12 g
- Cholesterol: 6 mg
- Total Fat: 2 g
- Fiber: 0 g
- Protein: 0 g
- Sodium: 32 mg

HOT COFFEE MASALA

Serving: 2

Preparation Time:5 minutes

Cooking Time: 10 minutes

Ingredients

- 2 cups water
- Two cumin seeds, or to taste
- One whole star anise pod
- 1/2 cinnamon stick
- 1 1/2 tsp. instant coffee granules
- 2tsps. nonfat dry milk powder
- 2 tsp. white sugar

Direction

1. Boil water in a saucepan; add cinnamon stick, star anise pod and cumin seeds, then stir. Lower heat to a simmer; cook while occasionally stirring for 3 minutes. Mix in instant coffee; let the drink simmer gently for 2 minutes longer. Add the drink in mugs. Strain out the spices; add in 1 tsp. Of white sugar and 1 tsp. Of nonfat dry milk powder in each cup, stir.

Nutrition Information

- Calories: 31 calories;
- Total Carbohydrate: 6.5 g
- Cholesterol: < 1 mg
- Total Fat: 0.1 g
- Protein: 1.2 g
- Sodium: 22 mg

ICED ALMOND MILK NUTELLA® LATTE

Serving: 1

Preparation Time: 5 minutes

Cooking Time: 35 minutes

Ingredients

- Two shots brewed espresso
- 1/2 tbsp. chocolate-hazelnut spread (such as Nutella®)
- 1/2 cup skim milk
- 1/4 cup almond milk creamer
- ice cubes

Direction

1. Mix chocolate-hazelnut spread and hot espresso in a big cup and stir till melted. Refrigerate covered for at least 30 minutes till chilled.
2. Add ice, almond milk creamer and skim milk to the espresso mixture; mix.

Nutrition Information

- Calories: 181 calories;
- Total Carbohydrate: 26.5 g
- Cholesterol: 2 mg
- Total Fat: 6.4 g
- Protein: 4.7 g
- Sodium: 147 mg

ICED CAPPUCCINO - LOW-CARB ALTERNATIVE

Serving: 1

Preparation Time: 5 minutes

Cooking Time: 5 minutes

Ingredients

- 1 cup unsweetened, plain almond milk
- 1/2 cup brewed strong coffee, cooled
- Three packets of granular no-calorie sucralose sweetener (such as Splenda®)

- 2 tbsps. cream cheese softened
- Four ice cubes, or as needed

Direction

1. Add cream cheese, sugar, coffee, and almond milk in a large plastic cup. Use an immersion blender to blend for about 1 minute until the cream cheese completely becomes liquid. Place ice cubes in a tall glass, then pour the blended beverage.

Nutrition Information

- Calories: 176 calories;
- Total Carbohydrate: 12 g
- Cholesterol: 32 mg
- Total Fat: 12.8 g
- Protein: 3.4 g
- Sodium: 251 mg

ICED COFFEE SLUSH

Serving: 12 servings (2-1/4 quarts).

Preparation Time: 10 minutes

Cooking Time: 10 minutes

Ingredients

- 3 cups hot strong brewed coffee
- 1-1/2 to 2 cups sugar
- 4 cups milk
- 2 cups half-and-half cream
- 1-1/2 tsp. vanilla extract

Direction

1. Stir sugar and coffee in a freezer-safe bowl till sugar dissolves. Store in the fridge till thoroughly chilled. Add vanilla, cream and milk; freeze. Several hours before serving, take away from the freezer. Chop mixture till slushy, then immediately serve.

Nutrition Information

- Calories: 202 calories
- Total Carbohydrate: 30 g

- Cholesterol: 31 mg
- Total Fat: 7 g
- Fiber: 0 g
- Protein: 4 g
- Sodium: 61 mg

ICED SKINNY HAZELNUT LATTE

Serving: 4

Preparation Time: 5 minutes

Cooking Time: 10 minutes

Ingredients

- 3 cups fat-free milk, divided
- 1/4 cup hazelnut Belgian cafe coffee drink mix
- 2 tbsps. refrigerated hazelnut coffee creamer
- Crushed ice

Direction

1. In a big microwave-safe bowl, add 1 cup of milk. Uncover and microwave for 1-2 minutes on high till hot. Stir in drink mix till dissolves. Add the leftover milk and coffee creamer. Serve over ice.

Nutrition Information

- Calories: 135 calories
- Total Carbohydrate: 22 g
- Cholesterol: 4 mg
- Total Fat: 2 g
- Fiber: 0 g
- Protein: 7 g
- Sodium: 125 mg

RISH CREAM

Serving: 8

Serving: 8

Preparation Time: 5 minutes

Cooking Time: 8h5 minutes

Ingredients

- Three eggs
- 1 tsp. instant coffee granules
- 1 tsp. chocolate syrup (such as Hershey's®)
- 3/4 tsp. almond extract
- 1 (14 oz.) can sweeten condensed milk
- 1 cup heavy whipping cream
- 1 1/2 cups whiskey

Direction

1. Place almond extract, chocolate syrup, coffee, and eggs in a blender, then blend.
2. Add whipping cream and sweetened condensed milk in the egg mixture, then blend again.
3. Add whiskey in the blender; blend till smooth. Let chill for 8 hours or overnight before using.

Nutrition Information

- Calories: 397 calories;
- Total Carbohydrate: 28.2 g
- Cholesterol: 127 mg
- Total Fat: 17.2 g
- Protein: 6.9 g
- Sodium: 100 mg

RISH CREAM COFFEE

Serving: 4

Preparation Time: 10 minutes

Cooking Time: 10 minutes

Ingredients

- Eight tsp. sugar
- 4 oz. Irish cream liqueur or refrigerated Irish creme non-dairy creamer
- 4 cups hot brewed coffee

- Whipped cream

Direction

1. Add liqueur and sugar into four mugs. Add in coffee and stir. Add whipped cream to garnish and immediately serve.

Nutrition Information

- Calories: 152 calories
- Total Carbohydrate: 16 g
- Cholesterol: 0 mg
- Total Fat: 4 g
- Fiber: 0 g
- Protein: 0 g
- Sodium: 5 mg

ISLAND SPICE COLD BREW

Serving: 2

Preparation Time: 5 minutes

Cooking Time: 5 minutes

Ingredients

- 8 oz. Gevalia® Cold Brew Concentrate - Vanilla, divided
- 2 oz. sweetened condensed milk
- 2 oz. half-and-half
- 1/8 tsp. ground cardamom
- 1/8 tsp. ground cinnamon
- ice cubes

Direction

1. Add half-and-half and sweetened condensed milk into a pitcher or a small measuring cup. Whisk in cinnamon and cardamom till blended and smooth.
2. Add ice cubes in mugs. Into each cup, pour in 4 oz. of cold brew concentrate. Over the back of a spoon, gradually pour half of the spice mixture into each glass.

Nutrition Information

- Calories: 141 calories;

- Total Carbohydrate: 18.8 g
- Cholesterol: 21 mg
- Total Fat: 5.9 g
- Protein: 3.2 g
- Sodium: 76 mg

K.O. COFFEE

Serving: 3

Preparation Time: 5 minutes

Cooking Time: 5 minutes

Ingredients

- 2 cups cold coffee
- 16 ice cubes
- 1 cup milk
- 1/4 cup semisweet chocolate chips
- 1/4 cup white chocolate chips
- 2 tbsps. chocolate syrup
- 2 tbsps. caramel syrup
- 2 tbsps. hazelnut liqueur
- 2 tbsps. coffee-flavored liqueur (such as Kahlua®)
- 2 tbsps. confectioners' sugar
- 1 tbsp. real maple syrup
- Two scoops of vanilla ice cream
- 1/4 cup chocolate-covered espresso beans

Direction

1. In a large blender, combine maple syrup, confectioners' sugar, coffee-flavored liqueur, hazelnut liqueur, caramel syrup, chocolate syrup, white chocolate chips, semisweet chocolate chips, milk, ice and coffee. Briefly blend till combined. Add ice cream, then blend till smooth.
2. To suck up the espresso beans, add a wide straw. Add espresso beans and pour the coffee drink on top in a serving glass. Serve.

Nutrition Information

- Calories: 472 calories;
- Total Carbohydrate: 67.7 g

- Cholesterol: 17 mg
- Total Fat: 18 g
- Protein: 5.9 g
- Sodium: 80 mg

KAHLUACCINO

Serving: 4

Preparation Time: 5 minutes

Cooking Time: 15 minutes

Ingredients

- ¾ cup nonfat milk
- ¾ cup strong coffee
- ½ cup Kahlua, or Frangelico
- 3 cups ice
- 4 tsp. sugar
- Shaved chocolate for garnish

Direction

1. In a blender, mix coffee and mix. Add sugar, ice and Frangelico (or Kahlua). Puree till frothy. Pour into four glasses and use shaved chocolate as garnish.
2. Non-alcoholic variation: leave out the alcohol and add 1/4 tsp. of almond extract.

Nutrition Information

- Calories: 138 calories;
- Total Carbohydrate: 20 g
- Cholesterol: 1 mg
- Total Fat: 0 g
- Fiber: 0 g
- Protein: 2 g
- Sodium: 27 mg
- Sugar: 19 g
- Saturated Fat: 0 g

KETO BREAKFAST COFFEE

Serving: 2

Preparation Time: 5 minutes

Cooking Time: 5 minutes

Ingredients

- One egg
- 2 tbsps. virgin coconut oil
- 1 tbsp. butter
- 2 cups hot coffee
- One pinch of ground cinnamon

Direction

1. In a blender, place butter, coconut oil and egg. Add hot coffee, then blend for about 1 minute on low till combined. Transfer into a coffee cup, then top the froth with cinnamon.

Nutrition Information

- Calories: 207 calories;
- Total Carbohydrate: 0.6 g
- Cholesterol: 108 mg
- Total Fat: 21.9 g
- Protein: 3.5 g
- Sodium: 81 mg

Serving: 1

Preparation Time: 5 minutes

Cooking Time: 5 minutes

Ingredients

- 3 cups ice cubes
- 1 cup 2% milk
- 1 cup strong brewed coffee, chilled
- 2 tbsps. sugar-free caramel topping
- 2 tsp. vanilla extract
- 3 (1 gram) packets of granular sucralose sweetener (such as Splenda®), or to taste
- 1 tbsp. fat-free frozen whipped topping, thawed (optional)
- 1 tbsp. sugar-free caramel topping

Direction

1. In a blender, combine sucralose sweetener, vanilla extract, 2 tbsp of caramel topping, coffee milk and ice. Pulse to crush the ice till it becomes thick and smooth inconsistency. Add into a tall glass or a mug. Garnish with whipped topping and sprinkle on top 1 tbsp of caramel syrup.

Nutrition Information

- Calories: 304 calories;
- Total Carbohydrate: 53.2 g
- Cholesterol: 20 mg
- Total Fat: 4.9 g
- Protein: 8.3 g
- Sodium: 235 mg

MEXICAN MOCHA MIX

Serving: 1

Preparation Time: 5 minutes

Cooking Time: 5 minutes

Ingredients

- 3/4 cup baking cocoa
- 2/3 cup sugar
- 2/3 cup packed brown sugar
- 1/2 cup nonfat dry milk powder
- 1/3 cup instant coffee granules
- 3/4 tsp. ground cinnamon
- 1/4 tsp. ground allspice
- ADDITIONAL INGREDIENTS (for each serving):
- 1 cup hot fat-free milk
- One cinnamon stick, optional

Direction

1. Combine the first seven ingredients in a blender. Cover and process till a powder is formed. Place in an airtight container. Yield: about 2-1/4 cups mix.
2. For the mocha drink: Stir 1 cup of hot milk with 3 tbsp. Mix in a mug till blended. Add a cinnamon stick as garnish if preferred.

Nutrition Information

- Calories: 207 calories
- Total Carbohydrate: 40 g
- Cholesterol: 6 mg
- Total Fat: 1 g
- Fiber: 2 g

- Protein: 12 g
- Sodium: 172 mg

MOCHA CINNAMON COFFEE

Serving: 6

Preparation Time: 20 minutes

Cooking Time: 20 minutes

Ingredients

- 1/2 cup ground dark roast coffee
- 1 tbsp. ground cinnamon
- 1/4 tsp. ground nutmeg
- 5 cups water
- 1 cup 2% milk
- 1/3 cup chocolate syrup
- 1/4 cup packed brown sugar
- 1 tsp. vanilla extract
- Whipped cream, optional

Direction

1. Combine nutmeg, cinnamon and coffee grounds in a small bowl. Pour in water and follow the manufacturer's directions to brew. Place into a drip coffeemaker's coffee filter.
2. Combine brown sugar, chocolate syrup and milk in a big saucepan. Cook while occasionally stirring till sugar dissolves over low heat. Add in brewed coffee and vanilla; mix.
3. Spoon into mugs. Add whipped cream to garnish if preferred.

Nutrition Information

- Calories: 95 calories
- Total Carbohydrate: 21 g
- Cholesterol: 1 mg
- Total Fat: 0 g
- Fiber: 1 g
- Protein: 3 g
- Sodium: 43 mg

MOCHA COFFEE MIX

Serving: 64

Preparation Time: 10 minutes

Cooking Time: 10 minutes

Ingredients

- 1 1/4 cups instant coffee granules
- 7 cups dry milk powder
- 5 3/4 cups powdered chocolate drink mix
- 1/4 cup confectioners' sugar
- 1 3/4 cups powdered non-dairy creamer

Direction

1. Combine powdered creamer, confectioners' sugar, chocolate drink mix, milk powder and instant coffee in a big bowl—place in an airtight container.
2. Into a coffee mug, add 4 tbsp. Of the mixture, add in and stir 1 cup of boiling water. Serve.

Nutrition Information

- Calories: 116 calories;
- Total Carbohydrate: 14 g
- Cholesterol: 14 mg
- Total Fat: 4.9 g
- Protein: 4.1 g
- Sodium: 72 mg

MOCHA FIRESIDE COFFEE

Serving: 6 cups mix (96 servings).

Preparation Time: 10 minutes

Cooking Time: 10 minutes

Ingredients

- 2-1/2 cups powdered non-dairy creamer
- 2 cups hot cocoa mix
- 1 cup instant coffee granules
- 1 cup Ovaltine chocolate drink mix
- 1/4 cup sugar

- 2 tsp. ground cinnamon
- 1/2 tsp. ground nutmeg

Direction

1. Mix all the ingredients in a big bowl. Keep in an airtight container. Serve by adding 1 tbsp. Of mix to 3/4 cup of boiling water.

Nutrition Information

- Calories: 43 calories
- Total Carbohydrate: 9 g
- Cholesterol: 0 mg
- Total Fat: 1 g
- Fiber: 0 g
- Protein: 0 g
- Sodium: 20 mg

MOCHA MORNING DRINK

Serving: 6

Preparation Time: 15 minutes

Cooking Time: 15 minutes

Ingredients

- 6 cups hot brewed coffee
- 3/4 cup half-and-half cream
- 6 tbsps. chocolate syrup
- 7 tsp. sugar
- Six cinnamon sticks (3 inches)
- Whipped cream in a can, optional

Direction

1. Combine sugar, chocolate syrup, cream and coffee in a big saucepan. Cook and stir till the mixture is thoroughly heated and sugar dissolves over medium heat. Transfer into six big mugs. Use a cinnamon stick to mix. Add whipped cream as garnish if preferred.

Nutrition Information

- Calories: 116 calories

- Total Carbohydrate: 19 g
- Cholesterol: 15 mg
- Total Fat: 3 g
- Fiber: 1 g
- Protein: 2 g
- Sodium: 29 mg

MOJITO COFFEE

Serving: 1

Preparation Time: 5 minutes

Cooking Time: 5 minutes

Ingredients

- One fluid oz. sparkling water, or to taste
- 1 tsp. clear mint syrup
- ice cubes
- 1 tsp. white sugar
- One fluid oz. brewed espresso
- 1 tbsp. whole milk, or as needed
- Two leaves fresh mint, or to taste

Direction

1. In a tall glass, combine mint syrup and sparkling water.
2. Stir in sugar and two ice cubes. Place more ices into the glass.
3. Gently transfer espresso into the glass. Add milk and use mint as garnish.

Nutrition Information

- Calories: 45 calories;
- Total Carbohydrate: 9.8 g
- Cholesterol: 2 mg
- Total Fat: 0.5 g
- Protein: 0.5 g
- Sodium: 20 mg

NUTTY COCONUT COFFEE

Serving: 2

Preparation Time: 4 minutes

Cooking Time: 4 minutes

Ingredients

- 2 cups freshly brewed dark roast coffee
- 2 oz. coconut-flavored rum
- 2 oz. Frangelico or another hazelnut liqueur
- Gay Lea Real Coconut Whipped Cream
- Ground cinnamon

Direction

1. Combine coffee with liqueur and rum. Transfer into two dessert coffee mugs. Generously place coconut whipped cream on top. Drizzle with ground cinnamon. Immediately serve.

Nutrition Information

- Calories: 214 calories;
- Total Carbohydrate: 21.7 g
- Cholesterol: 17 mg
- Total Fat: 4.4 g
- Protein: 1.7 g
- Sodium: 29 mg

ORANGE & COFFEE MARTINI

Serving: 1

Preparation Time: 5 minutes

Cooking Time: 5 minutes

Ingredients

- Ice cubes
- 2 oz. strong brewed coffee cooled
- 1 oz. vodka
- 1/2 oz. orange liqueur

- 1/2 oz. hazelnut liqueur

Direction

1. Fill 3/4 of a tumbler or a mixing glass with ice cubes. Stir in the leftover ingredients till condensation forms on the glass's outer side. In a chilled cocktail glass, strain the drink, then immediately serve.

Nutrition Information

- Calories: 172 calories
- Total Carbohydrate: 13 g
- Cholesterol: 0 mg
- Total Fat: 0 g
- Fiber: 0 g
- Protein: 0 g
- Sodium: 2 mg

ORANGE MINT COFFEE

Serving: 2

Preparation Time: 10 minutes

Cooking Time: 10 minutes

Ingredients

- Two fresh mint sprigs
- Two unpeeled fresh orange slices
- 2 cups hot strong brewed coffee
- 1/3 cup heavy whipping cream
- 2 tsp. sugar

Direction

1. Place an orange slice and a mint sprig in 2 coffee cups.
2. Add hot coffee into cups. Beat cream in a small bowl till it forms soft peaks. Add sugar slowly; beat till it forms stiff peaks. Serve with coffee.

Nutrition Information

- Calories: 166 calories
- Total Carbohydrate: 8 g
- Cholesterol: 54 mg

- Total Fat: 15 g
- Fiber: 0 g
- Protein: 1 g
- Sodium: 20 mg

PUMPKIN FRAPPE

Serving: 5

Preparation Time: 5 minutes

Cooking Time: 8h5 minutes

Ingredients

- 2 1/2 cups unsweetened almond milk
- 1 cup pumpkin puree
- 1/4 cup stevia sweetener (such as Truvia®)
- 1 tbsp. pumpkin pie spice
- 3 cups cold coffee

Direction

1. Whisk pumpkin spice, stevia, pumpkin puree and almond milk together. Add mixture into ice cube trays and let freeze for 8 hours to overnight till firm.
2. In a blender, blend coffee and pumpkin ice cubes till smooth.

Nutrition Information

- Calories: 61 calories;
- Total Carbohydrate: 15.9 g
- Cholesterol: 0 mg
- Total Fat: 1.6 g
- Protein: 1.3 g
- Sodium: 201 mg

PUMPKIN LATTE MIX

Serving: 18

Preparation Time: 5 minutes

Cooking Time: 10 minutes

Ingredients

- 1/3 cup vanilla-flavored powdered creamer
- 1 cup pumpkin spice flavored powdered creamer
- 1/2 cup instant coffee granules
- 1/2 cup white sugar

Direction

1. Combine sugar, instant coffee granules, pumpkin spice creamer and vanilla creamer. Place the mixture in an airtight container.
2. Add 2 tbsp. Of the latte, mix in a coffee cup for 1. Stir in 1 cup of boiling water till dissolved.

Nutrition Information

- Calories: 74 calories;
- Total Carbohydrate: 12.3 g
- Cholesterol: 0 mg
- Total Fat: 2.6 g
- Protein: 0.2 g
- Sodium: 17 mg

RATED G MEXICAN COFFEE

Serving: 6

Preparation Time: 10 minutes

Cooking Time: 20 minutes

Ingredients

- 6 cups water
- 1/4 cup brown sugar
- 1 (3 inches) cinnamon stick
- One whole clove

- 1/2 cup ground coffee beans
- 1/2 tsp. vanilla
- 1/4 cup chocolate syrup
- 1 cup whipped cream

Direction

1. Boil clove, cinnamon, sugar and water over high heat in a large saucepan. Stir till the sugar dissolves, then take away from the heat. Mix in the coffee ground. Steep, covered for 5 minutes. Mix in chocolate syrup and vanilla. Use several layers of cheesecloth to strain and remove the spices and coffee grounds. Add a dollop of whipped cream, then serve.

Nutrition Information

- Calories: 103 calories;
- Total Carbohydrate: 19.8 g
- Cholesterol: 8 mg
- Total Fat: 2.4 g
- Protein: 0.8 g
- Sodium: 36 mg

RICH HAZELNUT COFFEE

Serving: 4

Preparation Time: 10 minutes

Cooking Time: 15 minutes

Ingredients

- 3 cups hot brewed coffee
- 1/2 cup packed brown sugar
- 2 tbsps. butter
- 3/4 cup half-and-half cream
- 1/4 cup hazelnut liqueur or 1/4 tsp. almond extract
- Whipped cream and instant espresso powder, optional

Direction

1. Combine butter, brown sugar and coffee in a big saucepan. Cook and stir till sugar dissolves over medium heat. Add in cream; stir, and heat through.

2. Take away from the heat. Add liqueur and stir. Transfer into mugs. Add whipped cream as garnish and dust of espresso powder if preferred.

Nutrition Information

- Calories: 383 calories
- Total Carbohydrate: 49 g
- Cholesterol: 38 mg
- Total Fat: 10 g
- Fiber: 0 g
- Protein: 2 g
- Sodium: 80 mg

SARA'S ICED COFFEE

Serving: 4

Preparation Time: 10 minutes

Cooking Time: 50m

Ingredients

- 4 cups freshly brewed coffee
- 1/2 tsp. vanilla extract (optional)
- 1/4 cup white sugar
- 1/4 cup boiling water
- 3 cups crushed ice
- 1/2 cup cream

Direction

1. Store coffee in the fridge for 30 minutes till cool. Chill four glasses if preferred. Add sugar and vanilla extract in the boiling water; stir till dissolves. Store in the fridge for 30 minutes till cool. Evenly pour chilled coffee and ice into four glasses. Stir in sugar mixture and cream to taste.

Nutrition Information

- Calories: 155 calories;
- Total Carbohydrate: 13.4 g
- Cholesterol: 41 mg
- Total Fat: 11.1 g
- Protein: 0.9 g

- Sodium: 22 mg

SKINNY WHITE CHOCOLATE CARAMEL ICED COFFEE

Serving: 1

Preparation Time: 5 minutes

Cooking Time: 3h5 minutes

Ingredients

- 2 cups cold coffee, divided
- 2 tbsps. sugar-free white chocolate syrup (such as Torani®)
- 2 tbsps. sugar-free caramel coffee creamer (such as International Delight®)

Direction

1. Add 1 cup of coffee into an ice tray, then freeze for 3-4 hours till solid.
2. Add in 6 coffee ice cubes and white chocolate syrup in a tall glass. Add in cold coffee and coffee creamer.

Nutrition Information

- Calories: 24 calories;
- Total Carbohydrate: 4.8 g
- Cholesterol: 0 mg
- Total Fat: 0.3 g
- Protein: 0.6 g
- Sodium: 29 mg

SPANISH COFFEE

Serving: 6

Preparation Time: 0m

Cooking Time: 0m

Ingredients

- 6 oz. coffee liqueur
- 6 tsp. sugar
- 4 cups hot brewed coffee
- Whipped cream and chocolate curls

Direction

1. Pour liqueur and sugar into 4 mugs. Add coffee. Place chocolate curls and whipped cream on top. Immediately.

Nutrition Information

- Calories: 135 calories
- Total Carbohydrate: 20 g
- Cholesterol: 0 mg
- Total Fat: 0 g
- Fiber: 0 g
- Protein: 0 g
- Sodium: 6 mg

SPICED COCONUT COFFEE

Serving: 2

Preparation Time: 5 minutes

Cooking Time: 15 minutes

Ingredients

- 2 tbsps. ground coffee beans
- 1/2 tsp. crushed red pepper
- Two whole cloves
- 1/2 (3 inches) cinnamon stick
- 2 cups water
- 1/2 cup coconut milk
- 2 tbsps. honey

Direction

1. Set a coffee filter into a drip coffee brewer, then mix in cinnamon stick, cloves, red pepper and ground coffee. Pour water into the water reservoir of the brewer. Set the coffee brewer on, then brew.
2. Meanwhile, gently warm coconut milk over medium-low heat in a small saucepan. Mix in the honey till it dissolves. Add the brewed coffee to the mixture. Stir, then pour the liquid into two mugs. Serve.

Nutrition Information

- Calories: 185 calories;
- Total Carbohydrate: 21.1 g
- Cholesterol: 0 mg
- Total Fat: 12.2 g
- Protein: 1.5 g
- Sodium: 21 mg

SPICED COFFEE

Serving: 8

Preparation Time: 10 minutes

Cooking Time: 02h10 minutes

- 8 cups brewed coffee
- 1/3 cup sugar
- 1/4 cup chocolate syrup
- 1/2 tsp. anise extract
- Four cinnamon sticks (3 inches)
- 1-1/2 tsp. whole cloves
- Additional cinnamon sticks, optional

Direction

1. Combine extract, chocolate syrup, sugar and coffee in a 3-qt. Slow cooker. On a double thickness of cheesecloth, place cloves and cinnamon sticks. Enclose spices by gathering the cloth's corners. Use string to tie securely. Place into a slow cooker. Cover and cook for 2-3 hours on low.
2. Remove spice bag. Serve with cinnamon sticks if preferred.

Nutrition Information

- Calories: 64 calories
- Total Carbohydrate: 15 g
- Cholesterol: 0 mg
- Total Fat: 0 g
- Fiber: 0 g
- Protein: 0 g
- Sodium: 10 mg

SPICED COFFEE WITH CREAM

Serving: 2

Preparation Time:10 minutes

Cooking Time: 10 minutes

Ingredients

- 1/4 cup evaporated milk
- 2-1/4 tsp. confectioners' sugar
- 1/4 tsp. ground cinnamon
- 1/8 tsp. vanilla extract
- 1 cup hot strong brewed coffee
- Ground nutmeg

- Two cinnamon sticks

Direction

1. In a small bowl, add milk and place mixer beaters. Cover and freeze till it begins to form ice crystals for 30 minutes.
2. Beat in vanilla, cinnamon and sugar till fluffy and thick. Transfer into two mugs; pour in the coffee. Add cinnamon sticks and nutmeg as garnish. Immediately serve.

Nutrition Information

- Calories: 55 calories
- Total Carbohydrate: 7 g
- Cholesterol: 10 mg
- Total Fat: 2 g
- Fiber: 0 g
- Protein: 2 g
- Sodium: 32 mg

SPICED GINGER COFFEE

Serving: 15 servings (2/3 cup molasses mixture).

Preparation Time: 5 minutes

Cooking Time: 5 minutes

Ingredients

- 1/2 cup molasses
- 1/4 cup packed brown sugar
- 1 tsp. ground ginger
- 3/4 tsp. ground cinnamon
- EACH SERVING:
- 1 cup hot brewed coffee
- Milk, whipped cream and additional ground cinnamon, optional

Direction

1. Combine cinnamon, ginger, brown sugar and molasses in a small bowl.
2. Add 2 tsp of molasses mixture in a mug for each Stir in 1 cup of hot coffee till combined. Serve with cinnamon, whipped cream and milk if preferred.
3. Cover in keep the leftover molasses mixture for up to 2 weeks in the fridge.

Nutrition Information

- Calories: 48 calories
- Total Carbohydrate: 12 g
- Cholesterol: 0 mg
- Total Fat: 0 g
- Fiber: 0 g
- Protein: 0 g
- Sodium: 10 mg

CARAMEL FRAPPUCCINO COPYCAT RECIPE

Serving: 2

Preparation Time: 10 minutes

Cooking Time: 10 minutes

Ingredients

- 2 cups ice
- 1 cup strong brewed coffee, cooled
- 1 cup low-fat milk
- 1/3 cup caramel sauce
- 3 tbsps. white sugar

Direction

1. In a blender, blend sugar, caramel sauce, milk, coffee and ice together on high till smooth. Transfer drink into 2 16-oz. glasses.

Nutrition Information

- Calories: 271 calories;
- Total Carbohydrate: 60.2 g
- Cholesterol: 10 mg
- Total Fat: 2.5 g
- Protein: 5 g
- Sodium: 249 mg

TOFFEE-FLAVORED COFFEE

Serving: 5

Preparation Time: 15 minutes

Cooking Time: 15 minutes

Ingredients

- 1/2 cup heavy whipping cream
- 1 tbsp. confectioners' sugar
- 1/2 cup milk chocolate toffee bits
- 5 cups hot brewed coffee
- 2 tbsps. butterscotch ice cream topping

Direction

1. Beat cream in a small bowl till it begins to thicken. Beat in confectioners' sugar till it forms stiff peaks. Add toffee bits into coffee; stir and allow to stand for 30 seconds. Strain and remove any toffee bits that still haven't dissolved—Transfer coffee into mugs. Place whipped cream on top and sprinkle with butterscotch topping.

Nutrition Information

- Calories: 242 calories
- Total Carbohydrate: 22 g
- Cholesterol: 52 mg
- Total Fat: 17 g
- Fiber: 0 g
- Protein: 1 g
- Sodium: 150 mg

TRADITIONAL IRISH COFFEE

Serving: 4

Preparation Time: 15 minutes

Cooking Time: 15 minutes

Ingredients

- Traditional Irish Cream:

- 1 cup So Delicious® Dairy Free French Vanilla Coconut milk Creamer
- 2 tbsps. So Delicious® Dairy Free Culinary Coconut Milk
- 1/2 cup organic brown cane sugar
- 1 tbsp. vegan chocolate chips
- 3/4 cup cold brew coffee (or drip coffee or espresso)
- Vegan Irish Coffee with Whiskey:
- 1 cup Traditional Irish Cream (above)
- 1/2 cup Irish whiskey, or to taste
- Cocoa powder
- Mint sprig, for garnish

Direction

1. Heat water to a low simmer in a double boiler. To the double boiler bowl, add organic brown cane sugar, Culinary Coconut milk and Coconut milk Creamer. Occasionally whisk till the mixture is very warm (not hot) and sugar dissolves.
2. Take the bowl from the double boiler; add in coffee and add in chocolate and whisk till fully incorporated. Refrigerate or use immediately.
3. For Vegan Irish Coffee, combine whiskey and Vegan Irish Cream in a jar and shake. Add 4-5 oz. in a glass filled with ice or coffee cubes if available. Add a dust of cocoa powder.
4. Release a mint sprigs' oil by smacking it and placing it on the drink.

Nutrition Information

- Calories: 285 calories;
- Total Carbohydrate: 46.6 g
- Cholesterol: 0 mg
- Total Fat: 5.2 g
- Protein: 0.3 g
- Sodium: 10 mg

TURKISH COFFEE

Serving: 5

Preparation Time: 5 minutes

Cooking Time: 5 minutes

Ingredients

- 1 1/4 cups cold milk

- 2 1/2 tbsps. finely ground Turkish-style coffee
- 5 tsp. white sugar, or to taste

Direction

1. Mix coffee, milk, and sugar in a saucepan over medium heat until the sugar completely dissolves. Cook until the liquid begins making bubbles. Leave on the stove for another 30 seconds, then remove from heat. Serve hot and enjoy.

Nutrition Information

- Calories: 48 calories;
- Total Carbohydrate: 7.3 g
- Cholesterol: 5 mg
- Total Fat: 1.2 g
- Protein: 2.1 g
- Sodium: 27 mg

ULTIMATE ICED COFFEE

Serving: 1

Preparation Time: 15 minutes

Cooking Time: 12h10 minutes

Ingredients

- Cold-Brewed Coffee:
- 1/3 cup medium-coarse ground coffee
- 1 1/2 cups filtered water
- Coffee ice cubes
- Two packets Sweet'N Low granulated sugar substitute
- Milk (optional)

Direction

1. Fill coffee ice cubes in a tall glass. Add in the cold-brewed coffee. Use Sweet'N Low to sweeten to taste. Add milk as preferred.
2. For Cold-brewed Coffee: In a glass jar, place coffee, add water, stir till combined. Cover and put aside for 12 hours or overnight at room temperature.

3. Use a strainer lined with cheesecloth, a fine sieve or a large-size paper coffee filter to strain the coffee. You can refrigerate the cold-brewed coffee for up to 24 hours in a covered jar. You can double this recipe.

Nutrition Information

- Calories: 21 calories;
- Total Carbohydrate: 5.4 g
- Cholesterol: < 1 mg
- Total Fat: 0.1 g
- Protein: 1.2 g
- Sodium: 33 mg

VANILLA-ALMOND COFFEE

Serving: 1 lb.

Preparation Time: 5 minutes

Cooking Time: 5 minutes

Ingredients

- One lb. ground coffee
- 2 tbsps. almond extract
- 2 tbsps. vanilla extract

Direction

1. As usual, prepare coffee. Add in coffee and extracts in a big jar with a tight-fitting lid. Cover then shake well—place in an airtight container in the freezer or a dark, cool and dry place.

Nutrition Information

- Calories: 4 calories
- Total Carbohydrate: 1 g
- Cholesterol: 0 mg
- Total Fat: 0 g
- Fiber: 0 g
- Protein: 0 g
- Sodium: 4 mg

VIENNEXICAN COFFEE

Serving: 1

Preparation Time: 10 minutes

Cooking Time: 10 minutes

Ingredients

- 1 cup hot brewed coffee
- 3 tbsps. whole milk
- 1 tbsp. heavy whipping cream
- 1 1/2 tsp. brown sugar
- 1 tsp. cocoa powder
- 1/2 tsp. vanilla extract
- 1/2 tsp. orange extract
- 1/2 tsp. ground cinnamon
- 1/8 tsp. ground cloves
- 1/8 tsp. ground nutmeg

Direction

1. Combine nutmeg, cloves, cinnamon, orange extract, vanilla extract, cocoa powder, brown sugar, cream, milk and coffee together till smooth in a big mug.

Nutrition Information

- Calories: 129 calories;
- Total Carbohydrate: 11.9 g
- Cholesterol: 25 mg
- Total Fat: 7.5 g
- Protein: 2.5 g
- Sodium: 32 mg

VIETNAMESE COFFEE

Serving: 1

Preparation Time: 10 minutes

Cooking Time: 10 minutes

Ingredients

- 2 tbsps. sweetened condensed milk, or more to taste
- 2/3 cup strong brewed coffee
- 1 tsp. non-dairy creamer (such as Coffee-Mate®), or more to taste
- 1 tsp. hot cocoa mix (such as Godiva®), or more to taste (optional)

Direction

1. Add in a glass some boiling water. Leave to sit for 1 minute to warm the glass. Remove water. Into the warmed class, add condensed milk and coffee on top. Stir in hot cocoa mix and creamer.

Nutrition Information

- Calories: 158 calories;
- Total Carbohydrate: 26.1 g
- Cholesterol: 13 mg
- Total Fat: 5.1 g
- Protein: 3.4 g
- Sodium: 65 mg

WHOLE30® CINNAMON COFFEE

Serving: 1

Preparation Time: 5 minutes

Cooking Time: 10 minutes

Ingredients

- 2 tbsps. ground medium roast coffee
- 1 tsp. ground cinnamon
- Ten fluid oz. hot water (200 degrees F (93 degrees C))

Direction

1. In a small bowl, combine cinnamon and ground coffee. Add in hot water. Let brew for about 5 minutes. Into a mug, strain the drink.

Nutrition Information

- Calories: 12 calories;
- Total Carbohydrate: 3 g

- Cholesterol: 0 mg
- Total Fat: 0 g
- Protein: 0.4 g
- Sodium: 15 mg

WHYNATTE

Serving: 1

Preparation Time: 5 minutes

Cooking Time: 5 minutes

Ingredients

- 1 (12 oz.) hot latte
- 1 (1.5 fluid oz.) jigger Jägermeister liqueur

Direction

1. Add the latte to a pint glass. Add the Jägermeister liqueur in a shot glass. Let the shot drop into the pint glass (shot glass and all). Serve.

Nutrition Information

- Calories: 214 calories;
- Total Carbohydrate: 21.7 g
- Cholesterol: 17 mg
- Total Fat: 4.4 g
- Protein: 1.7 g
- Sodium: 29 mg

WINTER WARMER

Serving: 2 servings.

Preparation Time: 5 minutes

Cooking Time: 10 minutes

Ingredients

- Two envelopes (1 oz. each) instant hot cocoa mix or 1/2 cup instant hot cocoa mix

- 3 cups hot brewed coffee
- 1/4 cup half-and-half cream
- 3/4 tsp. rum extract
- 1/4 cup whipped topping
- The ground cinnamon, optional

Direction

1. Whisk together rum extract, cream, coffee, and cocoa mix in a small saucepan till cocoa dissolves and is heated. Add whipped topping to garnish and drizzle with cinnamon if preferred. Transfer into mugs.

Nutrition Information

- Calories: 194 calories
- Total Carbohydrate: 29 g
- Cholesterol: 17 mg
- Total Fat: 6 g
- Fiber: 1 g
- Protein: 3 g
- Sodium: 125 mg

Now, you know quite a handful of coffee recipes. If you tried all of them, feel free to go around calling yourself an expert caffeine drinker.

As you may have seen going through the recipes, making coffee is as easy as falling asleep. You could blend and mix the ingredients mentioned and create your unique coffee by adding your secret ingredients. You could even name it after you if you like. There are almost zero possibilities of going wrong while making a coffee.

Another bonus of knowing these recipes is that you could easily replace the dairy or non-vegan sweeteners with the vegan alternatives of your choice and have yourself a perfect coffee. This cookbook is that simple but comes in very handy for making many different coffees.

Making coffee has no particular strict rules. Fortunately, all you use are simple kitchen ingredients and basic kitchen utensils to prepare these coffees. The beauty of making coffee is that you can experiment with them as much as you like and never really go wrong. You will always end up with a tasty drink in your hand.

Made in the USA
Las Vegas, NV
12 November 2022

59234553R00079